THE CONTEMPORARY
CHORUS

A DIRECTOR'S GUIDE
FOR THE JAZZ-ROCK CHOIR

THE CONTEMPORARY CHORUS

A DIRECTOR'S GUIDE
FOR THE JAZZ-ROCK CHOIR

by CARL STROMMEN

Alfred Publishing Co., Inc.
15335 Morrison Street
Sherman Oaks, California 91403

Library of Congress Cataloging in Publication Data

Strommen, Carl, 1939—
     The contemporary chorus.

     Bibliography: p.

1.   Choral music, Juvenile—Instruction and study.
2.   Jazz music—Instruction and study. I. Title.
MT915.S78   784.1   80-18172
ISBN 0-88284-111-4

CONTENTS

PLEASE NOTE:

Due to a printing error in this edition of *The Contemporary
Chorus*, please read pages 86, 87 before reading 84, 85.

CONTENTS

PREFACE

Contemporary popular music has undergone a remarkable transition during the last fifteen years. Sophisticated recording techniques, creative use of electronics and a loosening up and expansion of form, structure, lyric and presentation have all contributed to a music environment whose classification often defies description. Techniques and style that were once the domain of jazz, for example, have been reshaped and intertwined with material that finds itself in the "Top 40" and some "Top 40" material has cropped up in some of the most esoteric of jazz labels.

Out of this amalgamation has emerged a fair percentage of quality music that has found its way into the performance literature of school music programs. As a result, publishers have been motivated to license copyrighted material for school use and a whole new breed of composer/arranger/educator has surfaced providing music for a choral setting that is distinctly unique.

Although the true "jazz" choir is a rarity, it is the non-improvisational stylizations of jazz that have become a pervasive force in the approach to what is currently referred to as the vocal jazz ensemble. It is these techniques as well improvisation to which this book is directed.

Certain areas will not be covered. Vocal production, other than brief mention, would require volumes and is far better illustrated by listening and doing—so take advantage of the discography. Choreographic techniques, while an interesting addition to some types of production, are also not in the realm of this book.

Other than definition and examination, it is not the purpose of this book to pass judgment on the wide variety of contemporary popular music. Specifically, we are dealing with the presentation of this music in the educational setting, the performance and understanding of which will require knowledge which might be somewhat removed from the choral directors area of experience.

As musicians and educators, we owe it to our students to provide them with a wide variety of musical settings and styles. Exposure to the demands placed on the professional musician can be an eye opener. To this end I am grateful for the contributions of Don Heckman and Harvey Siders.

As a relatively new area of music education, the concept of a vocal ensemble performing in a variety of popular and jazz styles brings with it various opinions and points of view. To this end, I am grateful for the contributions of the music educators listed below.

This book, then, is in part a collection of the thoughts and experiences of professional musicians, educators, composers/arrangers and publishers, the refinement of which will hopefully present material that is both musically and educationally sound.

Doug Anderson
McMinnville High School
McMinnville, Oregon

Elliot Bean
Syosset High School
Syosset, New York

Joseph Crupi
Horseheads High School
Horseheads, New York

David Cross
Shoreline Community College
Seattle, Washington

Frank DeMiero
Edmonds Community College
Lynnwood, Washington

Bobby Jean Frost
McGavick High School
Nashville, Tennessee

Gene Grier
Drayton Plains, Michigan

Waldo King
Roosevelt High School
Seattle, Washington

Dr. Bert Konowitz
Teachers College
Columbia University
New York, New York

Ken Kraintz
Everett High School
Everette, Washington

Jack Kunz
Lake Washington High School
Kirkland, Washington

Fran Roberts
Commack High School South
Commack, New York

Jack Seligman, Director
Instructional Materials Center
Mamaroneck Public Schools
Mamaroneck, New York

Dan Schwartz
Waldwick High School
Waldwick, New Jersey

INTRODUCTION

Within the last ten years, the demand by music educators for contemporary popular music has been phenomenal. The interest in this music has cut across all levels (elementary through college) and all areas (instrumental and vocal). The most striking example of this demand is to be found in the dramatic growth of the stage band/jazz ensemble in the instrumental program.

During the late forties, musicians (many having been released from the service) with jazz and commercial experience began to enter the ranks of public education. They brought with them an expertise which was not available in the standard college training of the music educator, and they believed strongly in incorporating their unique skills into the instrumental music program. The initial resistance from the traditional music educator slowly gave way to the understanding that here was an area of music that was challenging, exciting and educationally valid. Today, there are more than 30,000 junior and senior high school stage/jazz bands in the United States. Just about every college of music includes jazz band and related studies within the overall curriculum. Some colleges, including the Eastman School, Miami University, North Texas State and many others offer full degree programs in Jazz Studies.

During recent years, a similar trend has surfaced in the vocal end of the school music program. The demand for compositions and arrangements that involve the techniques and stylizations of contemporary popular music has dramatically increased. The reasons for this parallel the development of the jazz band; an exciting and challenging idiom and the clear fact that the inclusion of such ensembles are highly motivating to students.

Although choirs singing in a "pop" style have been functioning for many years (in the style of Waring, Coniff and Luboff), the emergence of jazz oriented vocal groups is relatively new. As with the instrumentalists, the leaders of the vocal jazz movement have not found their training in the colleges, but have brought in their own expertise, developed their own programs, and, in some cases, composed and arranged their own material. Where the "pop" chorus of the fifties and sixties could easily model itself after an existing large group such as the Pennsylvanians, the jazz vocal ensemble has no models other than the concepts and techniques surrounding the idiom. There has never been a professional vocal jazz ensemble group of the size currently popular in the school situation (16 to 24 singers). Directors and students may look to smaller groups in the professional world (Singers Unlimited, Hi-Lo's, Lambert, Hendricks & Ross, Double Six of Paris, etc.), but it should be stressed that besides the size difference, the final sound produced by many of these groups is, in part, a result of the electronic wizardry of the modern recording studio and the "studio" sound is virtually impossible to recreate "live".

The vocal jazz ensemble, then, is unique in that its development has taken place within the educational setting, whereas the stage band evolved as a replica of its professional counterpart. It is within the educational setting that choral directors must look for their examples. Although there are presently choral directors scattered around the country who are successfully involved in this type of ensemble, the most concentrated pocket of activity at this time is located in the Pacific Northwest.

Since 1968, the Northwest Vocal Jazz Festival at Mt. Hood Community College in Gresham, Oregon has grown to the point where approximately 120 vocal groups participated in the last session. It should be made clear that these are not organizations singing light "pops", but jazz oriented groups, many of which are totally involved in all the elements of that idiom.

It is from groups of this caliber that directors and students must draw both information and inspiration. It is encouraging to note that with the growth of the vocal jazz ensemble the number of clinics and workshops dedicated to this type of choral setting is increasing.

Thanks to the efforts of the National Association of Jazz Educators, the Music Educators National Convention, The American Choral Directors Association and the educational publishers, the jazz idiom has been warmly embraced by the educational community.

Joseph Crupi, director of the Horseheads High School chorus, Horseheads, N.Y., sums up the movement:

> "Be brave and give it a try. Most directors are afraid to begin. Listen to current jazz groups. Be aware of choral backgrounds on radio and television. Familiarize yourself with pop and jazz records. Listen to jazz artists, vocal and instrumental, to learn about style just as you would listen to Renaissance or Baroque music. Be adventuresome. Have fun!"

Chapter One
WHAT IS A VOCAL JAZZ ENSEMBLE

The term vocal jazz ensemble applies to a vocal group singing stylized jazz material with an emphasis on improvisation. More than often, this title is assigned to groups not totally involved in the elements of jazz, but for lack of a better term, it has grown to cover the broad spectrum of pop-jazz-rock vocal ensembles.

The vocal jazz ensemble has a size limitation—usually between 16 and 30 members with 20 to 24 being the norm. The ensemble is presented in a stationary format with a minimum of movement as compared to the more heavily choreographed show and swing choirs.

Although larger choirs are certainly capable of performing music scored for the smaller jazz unit, the sheer weightiness of the concert choir can present some problems in intonation, particularly within the rich and sonorous harmonic structures typical of some jazz arrangements. Also, the larger group will not have the "snap" and feel of a smaller group, especially when dealing with highly syncopated rhythmic figures that are so prevalent within the idiom.

The vocal jazz ensemble will be performing music that is stylistically quite different from traditional literature, not only in sound, but in the actual approach to the written note. The ensemble will also be performing with a rhythm section and occasionally with added instrumentalists.

The vocal jazz ensemble, and to a greater extent, the show and swing choir, will have a more "entertaining" quality than the concert choir. The question of how far to go in this aspect of performance will depend on how the director actually perceives his group.

There is a certain audience appeal to the visual side of a performing group as long as it is done tastefully and does not take away from the music. Perhaps the most appealing feature of such an ensemble is the sense of enthusiasm and enjoyment among the members of the group. Such enthusiasm is infectious and can sweep an audience right out of their chairs. Forced smiles, cheerleader movements, inappropriate uniforms and a writhing conductor do nothing for the music and can be a definite turn off. The key is low on flash and high on musical quality.

The question of "proper" vocal production brings with it a flurry of opinions and ideas. Everyone has their thoughts on how best to produce the "correct" sound within the jazz style. And with every method of vocal production there are dozens of jazz and pop singers and

EXTENDED WORKS

King David	Arthur Honegger
Mass	Igor Stravinsky

PRE-TWENTIENTH CENTURY MUSIC

Cucú, Cucú, Cucucú	Juan del Encina
Quand mon mary vient de dehors	Orlando di Lasso
O filii et filiae	Volckmar Leisring
Lo, How a Rose e'er Blooming	Michael Praetorius
Amour, Partes	Claudin de Sermisy
Wohlauf, ihr Gäste	Erasmus Widmund

TWENTIENTH CENTURY MUSIC

Sound Canticle on Bay Psalm 23	Gregg Smith
Go Lovely Rose	Eric Thiman

JAZZ-POP-ROCK-FOLK

Another Blues	Lapin
As Long as We're Together	Mangione/Presti
Climbing Higher Mountains	Oliver Wells
Closer	Lapin
Cuckoo Sport	Lapin
Day By Day	Schwartz/Lapin
Ease on Down the Road	Smalls/Fry
Entertainer	Scott Joplin
Hair	Mac Dermott/Lapin
Here's That Rainy Day	Van Heusen/Lapin
It's the Time	Larry Schwartz
Opener Medley	arr. Lapin
What I Did for Love	Sondheim/Winzeler

groups to contradict whatever the text book version claims to be gospel. The best advice is to listen to the pros—both in the pop and jazz field. Listen carefully to what the studio singers are doing on TV themes and advertisements. Saturate yourself in the "sound" of these groups and experiment.

One of the greatest musical gifts you can bring to your students is the understanding and application of stylistic flexibility. The ability to successfully perform in a variety of stylistic settings separates the musician from the singer.

One of the most accomplished college groups in the country is The Miami Chamber Singers from the University of Miami, Coral Gables, Florida. The stylistic versatility of this fine organization is clearly shown in one of their tour programs. (See page 2.)

There are, however, some tried and true axioms that hold no matter the style. Breath control and support are basic to whatever style is being sung—traditional or otherwise. The basic fundamentals should be taught so that the student will be able to sing with an open, free and unrestricted vocal mechanism. To impose drastic changes on the developing voice can not only be physically damaging, but to do so is poor education, and education is what the whole thing is about. If and when proper vocal training is accomplished, adaptation to style will become a natural by-product. Vibrato, for example, is a natural part of the vocal mechanism. The nature of the selection will generally determine to what extent vibrato should be used (up-tempo jazz, rock, ballads, simple triadic or more involved harmonic scoring, solo sections, etc.).

Certain aspects of traditional diction will be way out of line when performing with the jazz vocal ensemble. Again, style determines pronunciation. To eliminate the flipped "r" from a Gilbert and Sullivan operetta would be as out of context as to include it in a contemporary jazz or popular selection. It would be stylistically incorrect to sing an Appalachian folk song as one might approach an operatic aria. In other words, sing in the vernacular and be true to the style and song. Remember the last time you heard an opera "star" attempt to sing a popular song. It simply sounds wrong, as wrong as a pop or jazz singer attempting to sing an aria. In both cases, the learned or acquired vocal techniques become intrusive on the stylistic nature of the selection. Though musicianship permits one to move easily between styles. As more jazz oriented octavos become available, you will be exposed to inflection and articulation markings that have long been a part of the instrumentalists vocabulary, and the jazz singers natural state of vocal production. Since traditional notation cannot possibly accommodate these various inflections, a somewhat standardized explanation is provided below.

Proposed Standardization of Vocal Jazz Articulation and Inflection Prepared by the National Association of Jazz Educators by a committee chaired by Dan Schwartz

SYMBOL	DEFINITION/EXECUTION	PERFORMANCE SUGGESTIONS
∧ (vertical accent note)	**VERTICAL ACCENT** –usually a quarter note –strongly accented –held for less than its full value but longer than staccato –usually 1/3 of a beat; sometimes 2/3, depending on text and rhythmic intent –ending consonants (e.g., t,p,k) are often used to stop the flow of air, resulting in a natural shortness of time value	–be careful not to increase the tempo when performing consecutive vertical accents –do not decrescendo
∨ (horizontal accent note)	**HORIZONTAL ACCENT** –held for full value, sometimes for 2/3, depending on text and rhythmic intent –often used in syncopated rhythms –often used when the eighth note is tied over the bar to the first beat of the next measure	–sung louder than an un-accented pitch –although some syncopated notes are written without a horizontal accent, they are usually stressed –in eighth note patterns, the horizontal accents should be sung without breaking the smooth melodic line –if possible, the horizontal accent should be preceded by an instant of silence in order to heighten the contrast from no sound to-accented sound
– (tenuto note)	**TENUTO** –held for full value, usually without accenting –melodic lines in jazz and rock music are performed in a legato style unless specifically notated. The tenuto most often serves as a reminder of the basic legato style in passages which have staccato markings	–perform with a feeling of "weight" on each note –successive tenuto markings should be performed with space between the notes

SYMBOL	DEFINITION/EXECUTION	PERFORMANCE SUGGESTIONS
	STACCATO –short (but not accented), not heavy, clipped, or detached –the staccato note is separated from other notes without losing its forward motion –often used in conjunction with a legato marking for contrast –all staccato sounds should be only one syllable –words (or scat syllables) sung staccato usually end on such consonants as t, p, d, or k, which act as stopping devices to insure precise articulation. The rush of air ("uh") which usually follows these consonants in open diction is not present	–the ending consonant MUST be closed
	GHOST NOTE –Muffled or indefinite pitch –may be applied to any pitch needing a very soft but rhythmically vital sound	–must have the feeling of forward motion –is executed by a small grunt in the throat, and by closing off the flow of air with the tongue on the upper palate –often sung with an "n" consonant, as in "doot N doo"
	DOIT (pronounced "doyt") –an aggressive, rapid ascending slide (or "bending" of the pitch) which is often followed by a rest –the duration and intervallic distance of the DOIT is variable (it can exceed several beats in length and can exceed the interval of an octave) –the inflected note is robbed of its pitch value –no individual pitches are heard	–sound the written pitch before sliding upwards –the starting point of the DOIT may be moved slightly forward or backward in time –a decrescendo will result if the sound is gradually closed off at its upper end. However, the forward aggressiveness of the line continues to the cut-off
	PLOP –a rapid slide down to a given pitch from a large interval above –the first pitch may be chosen from the underlying chord structure, or can be a random pitch, which can reach more than an octave above the second pitch	–both pitches may be accented –keep the first pitch as rhythmically close as possible to the second pitch, without sounding forced

SYMBOL	DEFINITION/EXECUTION	PERFORMANCE SUGGESTIONS
SHAKE	**SHAKE** –sound the inflected pitch and quickly begin a fairly fast and even movement between the written pitch and a higher pitch –the interval utilized may vary from a minor second to as much as an octave, though usually not more than a perfect fourth –the duration of the SHAKE depends on the note value –generally, the slower the tempo, the wider the interval, and slower the speed of the shake. It is not uncommon for the speed of the SHAKE to gradually increase as it nears its completion –the speed of the SHAKE is affected by the speed, style, and dynamics of the music. Short notes usually have faster, more narrow shakes than longer notes with shakes	–first establish the chord; then begin slowly, and gradually increase the speed between the two pitches –it may not be necessary to attempt a group synchronization of the SHAKE –generally performed with a crescendo
ASCENDING SMEAR	**ASCENDING SMEAR** –usually starts anywhere from ½ step to a minor third below, and slides into the written pitch, reaching it only at the last moment –do not rob the preceding note's time value –generally, the longer the note, the slower the ascending speed of the SMEAR	–all SMEARS should have the feeling of relaxation –a crescendo may be utilized
DESCENDING SMEAR	**DESCENDING SMEAR** –the inflected note is robbed of its full time value, and is approached from above –the interval covered is usually (with numerous exceptions) an interval of a major third or less –the length of the slide is relatively short	–all voices use the note immediately preceding the inflection as the beginning pitch –slide smoothly into the written pitch and avoid accenting the beginning of the inflection

SYMBOL	DEFINITION/EXECUTION	PERFORMANCE SUGGESTIONS
	FALL-OFF –a quick descending slide (which is usually followed by a rest) –the duration and interval of the FALL-OFF is variable	–a decrescendo is usually included, and may be ended with an "airy (breathy)" tone quality –if the desired fall-off is a rapid drop in pitch, a "cool, airy" sound ending in "uh" is attempted. However, if a longer drop in pitch is desired, the sound produced should be less airy, and end on a vowel sound
	ASCENDING GLISSANDO –an upward slide between two pitches –it is not necessary to define SHORT or LONG glissandos because the notes at each end of the gliss indicate the interval	–a crescendo is usually included in the gliss itself, and can be slightly delayed. The result is a slightly postponed upward rush to the second note
	DESCENDING GLISSANDO –a descending slide between 2 pitches –the reverse of an ascending gliss	–a slight crescendo is usually included in the gliss itself, and can be slightly delayed. The result is a slightly postponed downward rush to the second note
	FLIP –sound the first note and maintain its pitch until just before the second note. There is a rapid upward raising of the pitch, followed immediately by a rapid drop to the next note –this inflection should be used only when the words can be sung as a flip –choose the highest point of the flip from either the underlying chord structure or random pitches. The highest point is usually no more than a fifth above the second note (although examples exist of over an octave)	–the highest point and the second note of the flip are usually accented –do not begin the flip (which is a delayed inflection) any sooner than the last 1/3 of the beat –a rapid crescendo is usually included

TOTAL NUMBER OF SYMBOLS: 14

The inclusion of these inflection markings will continue to be a part of published arrangements and the choral director should become familiar with their use and application. The nuances of jazz vocal production can be so subtle that written illustrations are, for the most part, inadequate substitutions for what the ear is able to perceive. The intangible and elusive quality of this uniquely American musical idiom was not meant to be written, but to be performed with the ear and the soul as its guide.

HOW TO START

Most successful stage band directors require that all the players, with the exception of guitar, piano and electric bass, be members of the concert band. The rational for this requirement is obvious—they will be playing many more times a week and therefore be developing their skills more than the non-participant. They will also be the students with the most dedication and enthusiasm. No less a requirement should be made for the singer who wishes to join the vocal jazz ensemble—draw from the larger concert choir. Unless you have a fresh crop of students in your choir, you will generally know the students who will be able to produce the quality and quantity of sound you will need. You will want students who have above average reading ability, flexibility, some sense of the jazz feel and the desire and enthusiasm to make the jazz vocal ensemble the exciting musical organization it can be.

As with any new performing group in the school setting, there will be scheduling problems. Until this new group is firmly established and recognized you may have to meet outside of the regular school day and on a somewhat limited basis (another reason for enthusiasm and reading ability). With a small group, however, there might be a common free period to all the members. Another possibility is to discuss with the guidance counselors the feasibility of rescheduling some of the members' classes so as to arrive at a common free period.

How about the teacher? Is he or she prepared to go full steam into the jazz vocal ensemble? Perhaps your interest has been sparked by what you have heard in surrounding school districts. If this is the case, pick the brains of your neighboring choral directors—invite them to bring their groups to your school. If there is little or no local activity in vocal jazz, contact the following organizations for further information:

American Choral Directors Association (ACDA)
P. O. Box 5310
Lawton, Oklahoma 73504

Music Educators National Conference (MENC)
1902 Association Drive
Reston, Virginia 22091

National Association of Jazz Educators (NAJE)
P. O. Box 724
Manhattan, Kansas 66502

For more immediate and detailed information concerning the vocal
jazz ensemble, write to:

Gene Grier, Committee Chairman
Vocal Jazz & Show Choirs
c/o 'PoP'pourri Unlimited
P. O. Box 307
Drayton Plains, Michigan 48020

All summer clinics relating to vocal jazz are listed in the Spring issue of
the ACDA Journal.

The type of music you choose will depend on the abilities and in-
terests of your particular group. But how do you find the "right"
music? Check with your fellow directors—see what has been successful for them under similar circumstances. Listen to the promotional recordings provided by the various publishing companies.
Attend as many reading sessions, clinics and workshops as possible.
Get to "know" the publishers who include jazz oriented, popular and
rock material in their catalogues. Below is a listing of publishers with
proven success.

Alfred Publishing Co.
15335 Morrison Street
Sherman Oaks, CA 91403

Campus Music Service
P. O. Box AA
Hawthorne, CA 90250

Creative Jazz Composers
P. O. Box 467
Bowie, MD 20715

Jenson Publications
2880 So. 171st Street
New Berlin, WI 53151

Kendor Music, Inc.
Delevan, NY 14042

Scott Music Publishing
P. O. Box 148
Hollywood, CA 90028

Creative World Music Pub.   Shawnee Press
P. O. Box 35216   Delaware Water Gap
Los Angeles, CA 90035   PA 18327

Hal Leonard Publications   Vortex Music, Inc.
8112 W. Bluemound Road   Distributed by
Milwaukee, WI 53213   Hal Leonard

Hinshaw Music, Inc.
P. O. Box 470
Chapel Hill, NC 27514

The vocal jazz ensemble can be one of the most exciting and energetic additions to any choral situation. Its value musically, educationally and in terms of public relations will be a plus to you, your group and to the entire music department.

Chapter Two
STYLISTIC ELEMENTS —HARMONY

I n an analysis of any period or style of music, a variety of rules and guidelines can be extracted that demonstrate how a particular "sound" is achieved. What determines the Baroque is often inconsistant with Romanticism and each is distinctly recognizable within a few measures of performance. We make general associations with the overall "sound" of a selection. No less can be said for the many stylistic divisions found in popular and jazz music. The sound of a Dixieland arrangement is a far cry from Bop as is the big band sound of Benny Goodman as compared to the arrangements of Gil Evans—yet all these examples fall within the realm of "jazz". These "sounds" are partially due to the voicing and harmonic structure of the arrangement, and it is what distinguishes a Gene Puerling arrangement (more complex) from a Carpenter arrangement (less complex).

It is the term harmonic complexity that causes some choral directors unnecessary concern. When placed in perspective and within the broad spectrum of choral literature, the difficulties, imagined or real, associated with "jazz" harmonies become far less imposing and more realistic in terms of performance. The harmonies of Bach are more involved than those of a familiar folk song and the harmonies of Stravinsky are more complex than Bach's, and most twentieth century literature will display harmonic structures far more complicated than those associated with jazz.

What is important for the choral director is that much of what is considered jazz by way of stylized harmonic structure is very often dependant on chordal substitutions, extensions and altered progressions. These techniques are not limited to only jazz, nor are these harmonic techniques a requirement for music to be called "jazz." If we analyze various harmonic techniques we will begin to see "clues" to look for when examining a choral work for consideration for programming. An understanding of the style will also help us in developing rehearsal plans and technique.

To illustrate these techniques, we will take the familiar *Twinkle, Twinkle* from a "less complex" to a "more complex" harmonic arrangement. The first example is written in a basic and traditional four part structure.

Ex. 1

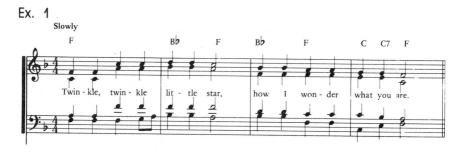

In the next example (Ex. 2), *Twinkle* is still written in four parts, but some of the harmonies have changed. Some of the F chords have become Am⁷ and Fma⁷ and the B♭ chords have become Gm⁷ and B♭ma⁷. What has happened here is that certain chords have been *substituted** for the basic chord. The resulting sound has a particular "edge" to it that lends itself to more of a jazz or pop sound than our original example.

Ex. 2

* The Am⁷ is really an Fma⁷(9) without the F root. The Gm⁷ chord, as the relative minor of the original B♭, acts as an appropriate substitute and the major 7 is added to the existing original B♭ triad in measure 2.

In Example 3, the entire *Twinkle* phrase is written in parallel fourths, a sound which has an open quality different from our last example. You will notice that while the soprano, alto and bass lines remain essentially the same in both examples, the tenor line has been lowered in this example by one full step.

Ex. 3

Example 4 expands on the area of substitutions (the opening chord is Bm⁷♭⁵), adds a fifth and sixth voice where necessary to handle the extended harmonies and provides some limited inner voice movement.

Ex. 4

In Example 5, the substitutions are further expanded and the inner voice movement is increased.

Ex. 5

The previous "Twinkle" examples were scored for four parts with occasional divisi where harmonic extensions demanded it. For the most part, thicker harmonic structures are employed in slower, ballad type selections. Where the tempos are faster and the rhythms more syncopated, lines tend to be thinned out allowing the individual lines to flow more easily.

Besides the addition of new and more extended harmonies and moving lines, a jazz sound is developed by how the lines are voiced. This voicing can make a distinct difference in the "sound" of an arrangement. The next example shows a four part phrase in what is called "open" voicing.

Ex. 6

By moving the voices closer together and tightening their texture (closed voicing) we get a sound more typical to what may be associated with a jazz arrangement.

Ex. 7

For added color and interest, arrangers often combine both styles. The next example uses both open and closed voicings as well as some interior movement.

Ex. 8

When an arranger eliminates the tenor part, the resultant sound is a bit more harsh, but lighter in weight.

Ex. 9

In the next 2-part example, the overall sound is a bit more flexible and will flow more smoothly, particularly at a faster tempo.

Ex. 10

The previous harmonic examples are generally associated with a pop or jazz "sound". As was mentioned, these techniques are to be found in other musical styles and by no means make a piece of music jazz. Extensions, substitutions and altered progressions evolved primarily because jazz players and singers found improvisation more challenging when faced with a set of "changes" (chord changes) more involved than what was originally written for a given tune, such as the previous "twinkle" example. This can be further illustrated through the simple I – IV – V^7 12 measure blues progression.

As the chords are played, sing the note "F" throughout the entire progression.

Ex. 11

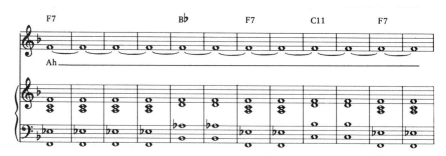

The next two examples illustrate how the introduction of a set of intermediate changes between the basic I – IV – V progression, can change the whole character of the blues. These changes also extend the potential for more intricate improvisation. You will notice that, holding the tone "F" becomes more difficult as the harmonic base becomes more involved.

Ex. 12

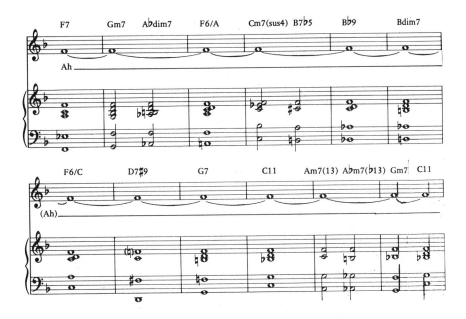

Ex. 13

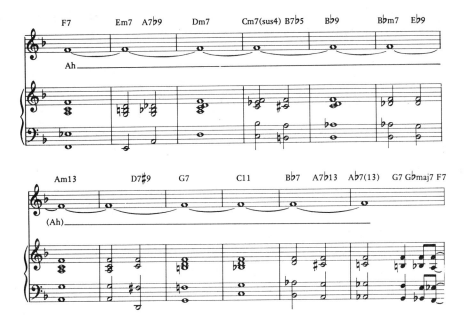

As these altered progressions became more a part of small group instrumental jazz, composers and arrangers began to incorporate them into big band and vocal arrangements. What is important is that while the melodic lines remained essentially as written ("Twinkle" and our lonely "F" tone), the underlying harmonic structure was subject to all kinds of interesting revisions.

These techniques for which there is a historical as well as a musical reason are prevalent in current vocal scores. The aspiring director of a vocal jazz ensemble should not be any more concerned about the "complexities" of jazz oriented harmonies than he would over a Bach chorale.

When choosing music for performance, the director should be aware and concerned about the judicious use of the harmonic techniques discussed. Some arrangers try to "out jazz" one another by cramming every known substitution, alteration and extension known to man into every measure of a tune—usually at the expense of range, line, voice leading and musical integrity. Is it reasonable for your ensemble to handle eight part divisi sections? Does such a divisi make any musical sense or is the arranger saying "look what I can do." How good are your singers' ears—can they maintain pitch comfortably in three or four part cluster voicings? Are the harmonies true to the nature of the selection or have they been capriciously or awkwardly selected just to get a certain sound.

The harmonic techniques associated with jazz and some pop material are only a part of the overall "sound". As we will see in the next chapter, it is the rhythms of jazz that usually present the most problems for the novice vocal jazz ensemble.

Chapter Three
STYLISTIC ELEMENTS
—RHYTHM

T he key to a successful jazz ensemble (vocal or instrumental), is how well the group interprets the pulse of the jazz "feel." In all styles and periods of musical performance, subtleties of interpretation are important and add to the overall effectiveness of the music. In jazz and rock, interpretive skills not only add to the quality of performance but are an essential part of the music. In "classical" music, if the performer plays the pitches and rhythms as indicated by the composer, the music will sound correct. It may lack certain interpretive qualities, but it will be musically correct. In the performance of a jazz selection, if the rhythms are played as written the music will sound stilted and wrong. The difficulty is that the subtleties of jazz cannot be accurately notated and to attempt to do so would result in a score that would appear incredibly complex and would still remain inadequate. It is for this reason that articulation markings and other helpful written "hints" are cropping up in jazz and rock oriented octavos with the assumption that the conductor can more accurately verbalize to students the composer/arrangers intent.

Many octavos will describe a selection by stating "jazz" or "jazz feel" or "swing," "rock," "bossa nova," "folk rock," or "latin feel." What this basically means is how to approach the eighth note.

Whenever the indication is "jazz" or "swing," the eighth note should be interpreted as the first and third beats of a triplet.

Ex. 1

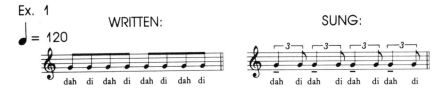

By delaying the second eighth note ever so slightly and approaching the notes in a legato fashion, that easy swing feeling so typical to jazz is established.

Example 2 from *Sing a Simple Song* should be sung as notated in Example 3.*

A similar feel should be established in *Alone and Blue* by Ken Kraintz. Example 4 shows the composition as written—Example 5 shows how it should be interpreted.

---

* Unless otherwise noted, all musical examples cited in this text are composed by Carl Strommen and © Copyright by Alfred Publishing Co., Inc., and are used with the permission of the publisher.

Ex. 4

ALONE AND BLUE

$\bullet$ = 120

Swing feel

Ex. 5

The jazz or swing feel is sometimes notated as in Example 6.

Ex. 6

Although this looks different than the eighth note notation, if it is to be performed with a jazz feel, it will still be sung as indicated below (Example 7).

Ex. 7

doo   doo doo   doo doo   doo doo   doo   doo   doo   doo doo   doo   doo

This excerpt in 3/4 time from *Have a Good Day* is an example of the dotted 8th—16th jazz notation. Notice the drum part. This is an example of the jazz feel in 3/4 with a pulse on the 2nd half of each beat.

Ex. 8

HAVE A GOOD DAY

(S.A.T.B with combo and optional Instrumentalists)

Relaxed Jazz Waltz (♩=120-132)

CARL STROMMEN

The correct way to sing this would be:

Ex. 9

Have you heard__ the news to-day? Have you heard__ that things are all - right?_____

The ♩ ♪ approach to the eighth note may be used comfortably at moderate tempos (♩ = 72–170). If the tempo is slower than ♩ = 72, the triplet feel becomes more difficult to hold together (slow Basie type arrangements are probably the most difficult to manage for the student instrumentalist and vocalist). As the tempo increases (over ♩ = 170), the eighth notes tend to "flatten" out and become more even. The following example is a "scat" chorus based on "rhythm" changes (chord changes to the song *I Got Rhythm*) at a tempo of ♩ = 280. Try playing or singing this line at a variety of tempos. As the tempo increases it will be physically impossible to maintain the ♩♪ feel.

Ex. 10

We have previously stated that stylistic descriptions at the beginning of a composition gave an indication to how the eighth note should be interpreted. Aside from the interpretation of the eighth note based on the description of the selection, the indication of articulation symbols may also aid the performer in achieving the correct "feel." The most common symbols are:

— (tenuto)—long sound

• (staccato)—short crisp sound

➤(accent)—stressed or louder sound, full value.
    A short accent would be marked ⋏ .

These articulation symbols are primarily involved with the rhythmic attack of the note and should not be confused with the other various inflection markings shown on page 00, which are unique to jazz performance.

In jazz vocal styles which tend to mirror big band figures, these articulation symbols can be particularly helpful. *One Thought On My Mind*, by Ken Kraintz is an example of such writing. The articulated rhythmic pattern is indicated below each measure.

Ex. 11

A selection that is described as Rock, Disco, Bossa Nova or any other Latin derivative treats its rhythms exactly as written. They are only affected by accents and inflection markings.

Where the "jazz" or "swing" pulse has an underlying pulse of "4" with the accent on 2 and 4,

Ex. 12

♩ = 132

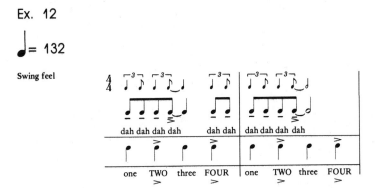

the Rock and Latin feel has an underlying pulse of "8" with the accents on each beat (these may shift, particularly in some Latin rhythms). Again the rhythms are played strictly as written and the articulation sound is closer to "dot" than the jazz legato "dah."

Ex. 13

♩ = 132

Some rock rhythms can be visually quite intricate, particularly when written in a "double-time" feel (the rhythms seem to be traveling twice as fast as the tempo marking). Since these rhythms are performed strictly as written, they can be easily subdivided especially with the constant reminder of that persistant "8" pulse. Note the tempo marking of the next example.

Ex. 14

The *Wind of Life* is described as a "Relaxed Bossa-nova." Being a Latin derivative, it retains the "8" pulse. Being a Bossa-nova, it will have a more legato feel than a Rock type selection might have. Notice the marcato markings at A6. If this were a "Rock feel" type piece, those quarter notes would have a tendency to be sung clipped and short. Also, take notice of the drum part. This is the standard Bossa-nova rhythm.

Ex. 15   WIND OF LIFE

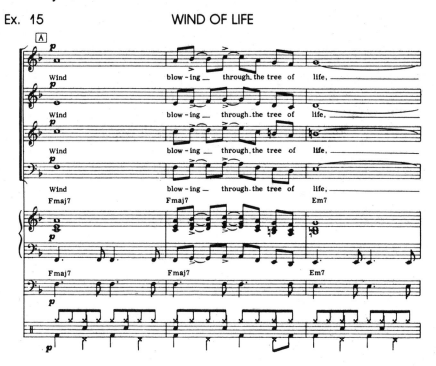

Where the rhythmic "feel" is not implied in the sung line, the accompanist and/or rhythm section must maintain the intended pulse. (The rhythm section will be discussed at length in a later chapter.) This situation is illustrated in *New Bossa* where the long whole and half note phrases must "float" over, and be supported by, the accompanying instrumentalists. Again, being a Bossa-nova, the pulse here is even eights. The piano solo at B11 must be consistant in pulse; to slip into a "4" pulse will not only sound completely wrong, it will also give the illusion of cutting the tempo in half.

Ex. 16   NEW BOSSA

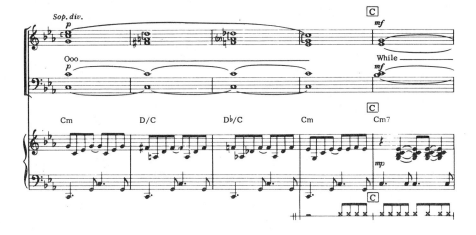

While the harmonies of some contemporary popular and jazz music may be accomplished with relatively little difficulty by reading the written note, the rhythms of the idiom are not so easily accomplished.

As was illustrated, what you see is not what you get. A contradiction perhaps, but true. The subtleties of jazz rhythms cannot be adequately notated, but with the aid of articulation and inflection markings, the rhythmic "feel" of jazz can be developed.

It has been said that a jazz musician of equal technical ability can more easily adapt to a symphonic or chamber situation than can a "classical" musician placed in a jazz environment. Whether this is entirely true is subject to debate and would make an interesting study, but the theory has probably been formulated in reference to each musicians approach to rhythm.

Once again, listening is the greatest teacher. Immerse yourself in quality popular music, rock and jazz. More than just the notes, try to involve yourself in that elusive word, "feel"—that pulse of the music that consistantly defies notation.

Chapter Four

THE
RHYTHM
SECTION

Most contemporary vocal arrangements will have rhythm section parts included in the published octavo, and some will include optional instrumental parts. Although the instrumental parts are not necessarily written as an integral part of the arrangement, their addition will add to the interest and excitment of the selection.

For many choral directors, this might be the first time they will be involved with instrumentation other than piano. If this is the case, and you feel uncomfortable about working with a full rhythm section and possibly additional horns, it is strongly recommended that you enlist the aid of and work closely with the jazz band director. His help in the initial stages of development of the jazz vocal ensemble can be invaluable and his exposure to the vocal department will not only broaden both your experiences but strengthen the appreciation of the problems and rewards you face daily. By working together, you will gain the respect and admiration of your students, colleagues, administration and parents. The result has to be a better product and a drawing together of the music department.

PIANO

It is the fortunate vocal director who has a competent accompanist. The details of this situation needs no explanation since all choral directors have been faced with this problem and well understand its implication.

The popular and jazz idiom present the pianist with a new dimension of style and performance. Most arrangers would agree that to write a piano part in the jazz or rock idiom in terms of making it "swing" would result in a part that would appear incredibly complex.

There is simply no way to adequately represent the "feel" of current jazz or rock piano parts in terms of contemporary notation. It is for this reason that the pianist should be well versed in the understanding of chord symbols. Not only will this free the pianist from reading parts that may be under or over written, but will give him the opportunity to get into the feel of the selection. If this is a problem, call on your jazz band director—he will probably have a pianist who can handle the situation. There are also numerous piano method books that explain how to construct chords based on letter names (see materials guide).

The pianist in the vocal jazz ensemble has a number of roles. He must be able to play the vocal parts when called for, provide the necessary rhythmic feel when playing as part of the rhythm section and improvise when indicated.

The following examples illustrate the piano in a variety of situations. In the first example from *Love Song*, the opening measures are specifically written (often the words "as written" will be indicated) with the chord symbols outlining the harmonic structure.

Ex. 1

LOVE SONG

(SATB/SAB with piano and optional combo accompaniment)*

CARL STROMMEN

In the same selection, the legato opening measures are contrasted by a light rock feel at letter B. Here, a simple rock rhythm is written as well as the chord symbols. At this point, the pianist has the chance to be rhythmically inventive. Although it is not necessary to read the written rhythms, the harmonic outline must be strictly adhered to.

Ex. 2

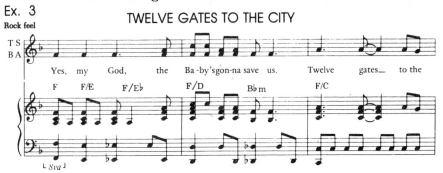

The ability to play variations on the rhythmic and harmonic outline is commonly known as "comping." To do this successfully the pianist must keep his eye on the written chord, the chord symbol and the flow of the arrangement. Most importantly, it requires "doing." The accomplished pianist will know when to stay within the written bounds and when it is appropriate to "comp" creatively.

In Steve Porter's *Twelve Gates to the City*, the piano part (R.H.) corresponds exactly with the vocal line, while the left hand part provides the rhythmic pulse. Without a full rhythm section this kind of piano writing is often appropriate. If a bass is available, the part should not be doubled by the piano. The resultant sound will be muddy and will not coincide rhythmically. By playing the part as written (with the vocal line) the intended rock feel may become stiff and stilted. Here, successful comping would probably loosen up the selection and make it "swing" as it should.

Ex. 3

TWELVE GATES TO THE CITY

Where improvised solos are indicated (either written out, marked with chord changes only, or both) it is hoped that the soloist (piano or guitar) will develop his own improvised line. Written solos may certainly be played as such, but essentially they should only act as a guide. In *All About The Blues*, the solo is written with the corresponding chord symbols. Notice the background voices sounding the harmonic structure.

Ex. 4

ALL ABOUT THE BLUES

All About The Blues - 10

Occasionally, "fills" (short, open piano solos) will be called for. They may be an interlude between specific sections as in *Bright Lights* by Ken Kraintz. Here, the four measures before C act as a "filler" between the text and a combination text and scat section a letter C. "Fills" may be improvised, but care should be taken to understand the intent. In this case, the piano prepares the voices with the note "A" in the measure before letter C. So, whatever happens during the fill, improvised or written, must have the voices entrance in mind.

Ex. 5
BRIGHT LIGHTS

A fill might indicate a modulation to a new key. In this case, care must be taken to lead the voices not only to their new note, but develop a sense for the new key. In *All About The Blues*, the piano is leading the singers from the key of D minor to the key of F minor. The final E in D3 prepares the chorus. If improvised rather than read, the purpose of the fill must be understood, otherwise the safe bet is to play as written.

Ex. 6 ALL ABOUT THE BLUES

A fill can often be one note. In *Sing A Simple Song*, the "A" octave in the R.H. at E5 acts as kind of a Basie "plink" that kicks the voices along rhythmically. To miss that note would seriously interrupt the flow of the selection. Again, the accomplished "comper" would instinctively recognize the worth of that one note.

Ex. 7

SING A SIMPLE SONG

Besides the skills required of the concert choir accompanist (reading, technique, interpretation) the pianist with the jazz vocal ensemble should develop the element of creativity; rhythmically and harmonically. He must be able to work as part of the entire rhythm section and not as a pianist accompanied by bass, drums and chorus.

Aside from the volumes of written material and methods available for the developing jazz oriented pianist, the importance of listening can not be over-emphasized. Listen to the giants of jazz piano: Bill Evans, Oscar Peterson, Hank Jones, Chick Corea, Herbie Hancock, Art Tatum, Erroll Garner, Bud Powell, Dave McKenna, Thelonious Monk, Barry Harris, Red Garland, Keith Jarrett, McCoy Tyner, Horace Silver and on and on. Listen to their individual styles, but listen to that intangible called "feel."

Listen to albums of singers with trio accompaniment: Tony Bennett with Bill Evans, Sarah Vaughn, Carmen McRae, Ella Fitzgerald, Frank Sinatra, and Mel Torme. Listen how the pianist compliments the vocalist without being intrusive.

GUITAR

The guitar is used essentially as a rhythm instrument when working with the vocal ensemble. Similar to the pianist, he must be able to read chord symbols and must be able to adapt to a variety of styles. To play in a twangy, trebly country style while performing a jazz selection is as out of place as playing in a mellow and subdued jazz style during a country piece.

It should be noted that the guitar is not an absolute necessity in the rhythm section, especially when the piano is present. There will be times when the addition of the guitar will be a welcome addition (amplified acoustic in folk selections, electric rock sound when appropriate, and occasional doubling of the melodic line for coloration) but, for reasons which will be explained, the use of the guitar should be used judiciously.

Guitar parts are almost always written as chord symbols. The slash marks indicate that the chord is played throughout the entire measure (measures 1 and 2, 6 and 7). Occasionally, specific rhythmic figures will be indicated. These should be played as written. In measure 3, 4 and 5 of the following example *Saturday's Child*, the guitar is directed to play the same rhythm as indicated in the piano part. Notice the figure in the last three measures. Here the guitarist is to hold the F chord for three measures. This is done by one strike of the chord and letting it ring for the duration.

Ex. 8

SATURDAY'S CHILD

One very important consideration when using the guitar with piano is the fact that there are often dissimilar chord voices between the two instruments. Although few problems will arise with triadic or seventh voicings, the difficulty becomes noticeable in extensions beyond the ninth and in cluster voicings.

The following example shows a D^7 ($\flat^9$, $\flat^5$) chord as often voiced by the piano and guitar. The resultant dissonance is obvious. (Guitar is written one octave higher than it sounds—for this example it is written as sounded.)

Ex. 9

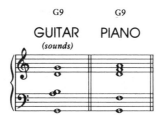

If the guitarist chooses to use cluster voicings, as in the next example, against a typical piano voicing of the same chord, the sound will be unclear and muddled, and will tend to sound out of tune.

Ex. 10

The solution to this problem is for the guitarist and pianist to work out the chord changes and voicings together. Where there seems to be difficulty in resolving what voicings to use, have one or the other play.

There will always be intonation problems between the guitarist and pianist (this situation may be particularly acute when using an electric piano). The guitarist should be constantly aware of intonation and make the proper adjustments when necessary. Temperature, humidity and old strings have a tendency to put the guitar out of tune and nothing sounds worse than the guitar out of tune with the piano. It will certainly not help the chorus either.

Another important point to consider is that every auditorium is acoustically unique and will react differently to amplification. So, always check amplified sound levels away from the stage. What might appear to be adequate in terms of volume and balance onstage very often will be completely different in the audience area.

Again, listen. All the method books in the world are of little value unless you hear what should be done. Who are they? Here are some to listen to: Freddie Greene, Johnny Smith, Barney Kessell, Joe Pass, Herb Ellis, Jim Hall, Kenny Burrell, Charlis Byrd, Al DiMeola, Chuck Wayne, Wes Montgomery, John McLaughlin, George Benson, and Larry Coryell.

THE BASS

Where the guitar is an interesting addition to the rhythm section, the bass is absolutely essential. It is the "bottom" and bulwark of the rhythm section and its function rhythmically and harmonically are so important that its absence will cause the rhythm section to literally "fall apart."

The electric bass is currently the most popular instrument. Most students now learn on the electric, whereas some years ago initial bass instruction was on the traditional acoustic model. Ideally, it is hoped that the player can handle both, an absolute necessity for the professional.

While the jazz (in 4) feel lends itself to the acoustic, the technical demands of rock bass figures are ideally suited to the electric.

As with the guitar, amplification levels are critical, especially when working with voices. Too much bass response will produce a "boomy" sound creating an undefined pitch. Too much treble will be harsh and overbearing. Levels should be predetermined so that dial turning is kept at a minimum during performance. Again check levels away from the stage.

Most published material for the vocal ensemble provides a part for the bass. And, as with the piano and guitar, the chord symbols are available for further reference.

Bass parts are sometimes incorporated onto the piano parts as in Ken Kraintz' *Bright Lights* (left hand parts—stems down). When incorporated into the piano part the composer/arranger usually indicates the notes he wants to hear. Since the bass sounds one octave lower than written, a bass player would have to play this part one octave higher.

Ex. 11

BRIGHT LIGHTS

Where the bass part is not specifically written, it can be extrapolated from the piano part and chord changes, as in *Many Songs Ago*.

Ex. 12

MANY SONGS AGO

(SATB with Piano)

CARL STROMMEN

Where specifically indicated, the bass parts should be played as written, as in this excerpt from *An Answer For Our Time.*

Ex. 13

ANSWER FOR OUR TIME

Besides playing a clearly defined line, the bass player should have a solid sense of time. Nothing can wreck more havoc within a rhythm section than a bassist whose time "floats" and is uneven.

As with the other instruments of the rhythm section, the best instruction is listening to the pros: Ray Brown, Ron Carter, Richard Davis, George Duvivier, Paul Chambers, Milt Hinton, Chuck Isreals, Scott LaFaro, Steve Swallow, Charlie Hayden, Eddie Gomez, George Mraz, Jaco Pastorious, and Stanley Clarke, are a few to choose from.

THE DRUMS

The drummer is the key to the successful rhythm section. Since he will have to provide a great deal of control over the vocal ensemble, the ideal drummer, rather than being a remarkable technician, should have a flawless sense of time. The rhythm section acts as an integrated support unit to the voices, not a section accompanied by voices, so the pyro-techniques young drummers are so eager to display are completely out when working with a vocal ensemble.

As with the amplified instruments, check the sound of the drums away from the stage. An overzealous drummer can completely wash over the sound of a chorus. I recall listening to a choir of 30 trombones with rhythm section. The low ceiling back wall of the stage was heavily curtained and the trombones were positioned in a semicircle with the drums set up to the extreme stage right. When the drummer used his sticks on the cymbals the sound completely obliterated that very large and potentially powerful ensemble. So, watch the use of sticks on cymbals, and encourage the use of brushes. If sticks must be used, they should be light with a medium weight cymbal.

The bass drum can be equally as hazardous. It should not be used to keep time (leave that to the bass) but rather to accent or punctuate ensemble figures. The potentially "boomy" sound of the bass drum should be reduced to a punctuating unobtrusive sound. The heads may be muffled and the front head may be removed.

The drummers role is low on flash and high on time and holding the entire rhythm section and vocal ensemble together.

As with the piano, bass and guitar, the drum parts can be written in a variety of ways. In the following example from *Get Together Now* by Sandy Feldstein, the drum part is thoroughly written and should be played as such since the part is reinforcing the vocal rhythms. Notice in measure 29 how the various parts of the drum set are indicated on the staff.

Ex. 14

GET TOGETHER NOW

Where there are changes in meter and pulse, the drum parts should be played as written. In *It's My Day*, the section before letter F is a jazz feel shuffle in 4. At letter F, the feel changes to 8 (rock feel). Here the drummer must be aware of that change in pulse. If he continues in 4 at letter F, it will sound awkward and wrong.

Ex. 15

IT'S MY DAY

When the tempo is consistent throughout and there are a minimum of rhythmic "cuts" among the ensemble and instrumentalists, a sample of the required rhythms may be indicated in the opening measures followed by "simile," repeat signs or the words, "drums continue." The "light rock beat" in *Sausalito Strut* is presented in the third and fourth measure only. It then becomes the drummers responsibility to maintain the feel and make any embellishments where it might be appropriate.

Ex. 16

SAUSALITO STRUT
(SATB/SAB with piano and optional combo accompaniment)*

CARL STROMMEN

A similar example is described in *Back Bay Shuffle*. The first two measures indicate "Shuffle—heavy back beat"—there is no need to continue a written part since the indicated feel will continue until 1 before C where the indication is a straight four feel with the drums playing on "closed H.H." (high hat).

Ex. 17

BACK BAY SHUFFLE

(S.A.T.B./S.A.B. with piano and optional combo)*

CARL STROMMEN

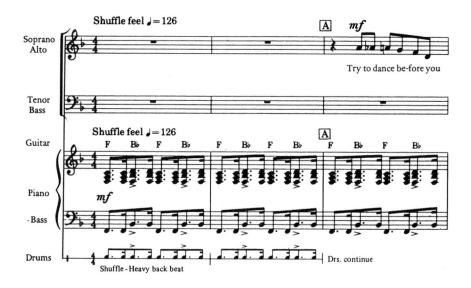

Occasionally, as in Ken Kraintz' One Thought On My Mind, the only indication will be "drums," "drums with sticks" or "with brushes." In this selection, the ensemble figures are so big band-like, that the drummer should have no problem—he simply can follow the entire score. One hint—the drummer and the bass player will not be able to turn pages while playing, so tape the pages of the octavo together and spread them out over as many stands as needed. Once they learn the music, they probably won't need the score anyway.

Ex. 18

One Thought On My Mind

(SSATB with Piano and Optional Combo Accompaniment)

KEN KRAINTZ

With the function and responsibilities of the rhythm section in mind, let us look at some further examples.

Saturday's Child includes both rhythm section and optional instrumentalists (trumpet, alto and tenor saxophone and trombone). The opening measures should be played as written. At letter A, the rhythm section is provided with a basic sketch that carries throughout the piece. As written, the rhythm parts are certainly adequate, but it is the arranger's hope that this sketch be treated as an outline from which the players can work, providing melodic and rhythmic embellishments where they seem appropriate.

Ex. 19

SATURDAY'S CHILD

(S.A.T.B. or S.A.B. with combo and optional instrumentalists)

CARL STROMMEN

In selections which contain jazz oriented harmonies, the rhythm section will have to be more skillful and careful in working around the sketch. In *Bright Lights*, the close, five part harmonies should not be interferred with by an overly exuberant rhythm section. Although variations on the rhythmic outline would be acceptable, extensions beyond the written chord might destroy the original harmonic intent. Also, since the harmonies are somewhat involved, it is absolutely critical that the pianist and guitarist work out the chord voicings before a full rehearsal.

Ex. 20   BRIGHT LIGHTS

Obviously, the rhythm section will be a critical factor in the success of the jazz vocal ensemble. Most likely, you will be using students who are in the jazz band and are used to pushing high energy instrumentalists. When playing with the vocalists, the instrumentalists will have to adapt to a different stylistic setting. As the director, you will have to know when to pull in the reins as well as when to let them have their own lead. Young instrumentalists who are being trained in a successful stage band program can be surprisingly mature in their musical attitudes. You should not hesitate to ask their opinions where you may have some doubts. As long as you maintain control, such student involvement can only help to promote the development of your ensemble.

Chapter Five

THE VOCAL ENSEMBLE WITH THE JAZZ BAND

U p to this point, we have discussed the vocal ensemble with the rhythm section and optional instrumentalists. Within the last few years, publishers have been producing arrangements where jazz band and voices can work together or independently of each other. The total effect of this combination can be quite exciting.

Some serious musical decisions arise in such a setting. For one, the melodic line will invariably be doubled between voice and instrument(s). The question of whether to have the lead line doubled is a matter of balance (will the horns overpower the voices), taste (is the sound of the lead line doubled between voices and instruments appealing and/or appropriate in this particular arrangement), intonation (no explanation necessary), or necessity (is it necessary for the instruments to help carry the vocal line). Experiment!

An example of this situation is shown in *Senses* by Marty Gold and Sandy Feldstein. In measure four (Examples 1(a) and 1(b)), the voices are doubled by the saxophone section in unison. If the sax's play subito, the combination should be rich and sonorous. If the sax's are still too overbearing, adjustments should be made in amplification, eliminate the number of sax's playing or eliminate the entire sax section while retaining the background figures provided by the brass.

Notice how the piano part in the vocal score is orchestrated in the jazz band score. Vibes double right hand (stems up), guitar doubles right hand (stems down).

Ex. 1(a)

Vocal score

SENSES

(S. A. T. B. with Combo and optional *Stage Band Accompaniment)

MARTY GOLD
SANDY FELDSTEIN

Ex. (1(b))

Jazz band
condensed score

Senses

MARTY GOLD
SANDY FELDSTEIN

Conductor

If the voices are doubled by the full instrumental ensemble, balance can be achieved by 1) making amplification adjustments, 2) reducing the dynamic level of the jazz band, and 3) reducing the number of instruments (for example, having one player in each section). If instruments are eliminated, harmonic considerations should be taken into account.

At E9 in *Wind of Life*, the brass are written with the voices, while the saxophones are playing a simple contrapuntal line beneath the melody (see Example 2(a)—stems down, treble clef). An effective sound at this point would be to eliminate the brass while retaining the sax line—which would not interfere melodically but would reinforce and enhance the harmonic flow of the voices.

Ex. 2(a)

WIND OF LIFE

Ex. 2(b)   WIND OF LIFE

A similar example is to be found at letter D of *Christmas Medley*. The sax's in Example 3(a) are playing in unison with the vocal line while the trombones are doubling the piano part in the vocal score in Example 3(b).

Ex. 3(a)   CHRISTMAS MEDLEY

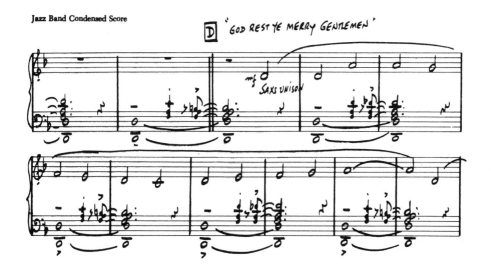

Ex. 3(b)

CHRISTMAS MEDLEY

Vocal score

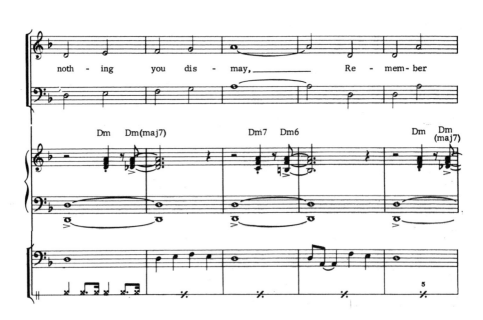

At letter F in *Christmas Medley* (Examples 4(a) and 4(b)), the full jazz band is playing with the vocal ensemble. The altered chord structure here (notice the divisi in the vocal part) will be quite effective with full vocal and instrumental ensemble only if the jazz band remains a notch below the singers in volume level. At G5 the tenors and basses are singing the line in unison while the first trumpet plays the same line two octaves higher over the full harmonic scoring of the band. It is not easy for the trumpet to maintain a subito level at such a high range—if this is a problem, drop the trumpet down an octave. If your trumpet player can handle the higher part and the overall balance between band and singers is successful, the effect will be stunning.

Ex. 4(a)

CHRISTMAS MEDLEY

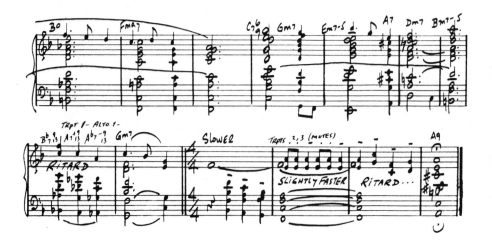

Ex. 4(b)

CHRISTMAS MEDLEY

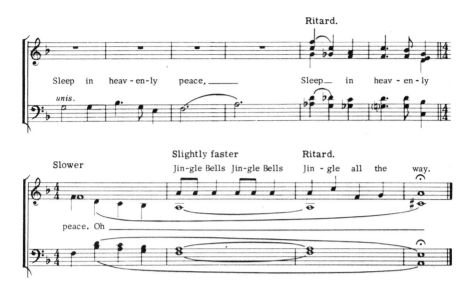

Although there are frequent unison passages between the voices and jazz band in these types of arrangements, there will occasionally be passages where the two scores don't seem to jibe. An example of this situation is a letter E in *Back Bay Shuffle* (Example 5(a) and 5(b)). What appears to be two separate arrangements at this point will make sense if you consider the jazz band part background "punch" figures over the vocal line. At E9 the sax's and trumpets double the vocal lines while the trombones complement the line with those eighth notes after beat figures.

Ex. 5(a)

BACK BAY SHUFFLE

Jazz Band Condensed Score

Cond. Sc.

Ex. 5(b)

BACK BAY SHUFFLE

Vocal score

Which way are you go - in'?___   It don't mat-ter an-y   more.

As in *Sausalito Strut* (Examples 6(a) and 6(b)), there will most likely be a solo or improvisational section in the band part that will coincide with the vocal arrangement. If the vocal ensemble has advanced to the point of group or individual improvisation, solo chorus' can be divided between instrumentalists and vocalists. If vocal improvisation is not possible, the pianist may play (written solo in choral part—or improvised) and share chorus' with members of the band. An improvisational section should be "opened up" or extended for as many solos as seems reasonable. When the last solo is being played, the director simply cues the entire ensemble to the second ending or next rehearsal letter. Notice in this example how the background figures at G are similar between the voices and instrumentalists.

Ex. 6(a)

SAUSALITO STRUT

Jazz Band Condensed Score

Ex. 6(b)

SAUSALITO STRUT

Vocal score

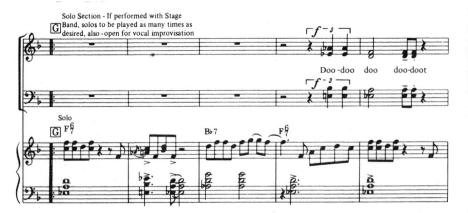

The vocal–jazz band combination can provide a unique dimension to any performance situation. And when the two groups "click," the effect can be electric.

The major problem will be balance. As has been described, this can be handled by proper amplification, adjustments in orchestration and physical set-up examples of which are given in the next chapter.

Combined rehearsal time can be kept at a minimum and scheduled only when both groups have properly prepared their parts.

Aside from the musical experience, there is no question that such a setting can be a definite "morale booster" for both the students and the directors and will display a solidarity within the music department.

Chapter Six

THE
SET UP
AND
SOUND SYSTEM

Obviously, the problem of balance is critical in any vocal–instrumental situation. The previous chapter demonstrated how certain balance problems were solved through alterations in orchestration. Equally important is how the vocal instrumental ensemble is physically arranged and the proper use of the sound system.

While show and swing choirs will be involved in more extensive choreography, the jazz oriented ensemble will emphasize the music and be presented with a minimum of movement on 3 tier risers.

From the basic groupings shown below (quartets, by sex and mixed) the director can creatively rearrange the vocalists for the most effective presentation, visually and aurally, of his particular group.

Ex. 1

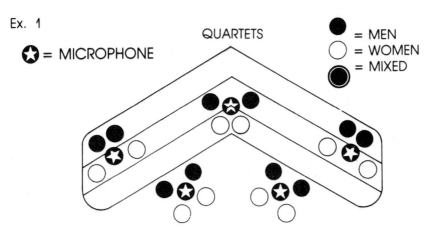

BY SEX

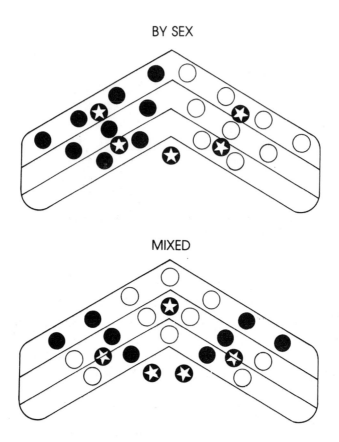

MIXED

The previous diagrams show microphones placed at various points among the singers. Proper placement for your group will be somewhat experimental, but generally with three or four singers on a microphone, the presence of the entire group will be greatly enhanced.

Microphones are available in a variety of designs and styles. The two most widely used mics are the *electrostatic* (also known as a *condensor* microphone) and the *dynamic.* These terms refer to the physics of their "pick up" mechanisms.

The electrostatic microphone is considered the superior unit as it has the cleanest sound and the truest fidelity. It is, however, delicate and cannot take much abuse. The dynamic microphone does not have the fidelity of the electrostatic, but it is quite durable.

Both the electrostatic and dynamic mics are available in three categories: *omni-directional, uni-directional* (also known as cardiod) and *shotgun.* These terms refer to their particular sensitivity (pick up) configuration.

OMNI-DIRECTIONAL

The pick up configuration of the omni-directional microphone is as description indicates—a full 360 degree circle around the microphone. Although considered to have the best fidelity, its sensitivity configuration makes it most prone to react to feedback (reflected sound) and extraneous noise.

Ex. 2

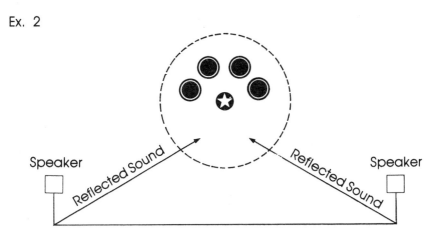

UNI-DIRECTIONAL (cardiod)

The uni-directional microphone does not pick up sound within a 360 degree range. The word cardiod, in fact, describes its heart shaped sensitivity configuration. Since it will not pick up sound at the back of the microphone (audience side), the chances of picking up reflected sound is greatly reduced.

Ex. 3

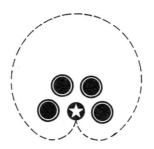

SHOTGUN

The shotgun is the only true directional microphone. The word "shot-gun" describes its pick-up configuration. Since it is able to focus in on a narrow area, it is particularly good in a situation with severe acoustical problems (extremely "live" hall). It is, however, somewhat unwieldy, quite expensive and does not have the fidelity of the omni- or uni-directional microphones.

Ex. 4

Considering all the alternatives, the most practical microphone for school use would seem to be the dynamic uni-directional (cardiod). Its "pick-up" configuration minimizes feedback, it is durable and portable, and it will provide more than adequate fidelity.

It is strongly suggested that you purchase *windscreens* for each of your microphones. They are simply foam covers which are fitted over each mike. They are ideal for outdoor concerts since they eliminate wind noise and are especially helpful for performers who tend to "explode" their words.

SPEAKERS

As with microphones, there are a variety of speakers. And as with microphones, you should look for quality, portability and durability. Most importantly, the speaker should have a projection configuration that will minimize feedback. What this means is that you do not want a speaker that will project up or down (thereby causing reflected sound from the ceiling or floor), but one that projects directly out to the audience. This configuration is best attained by the "column" type speaker (see Example 5).

Ex. 5

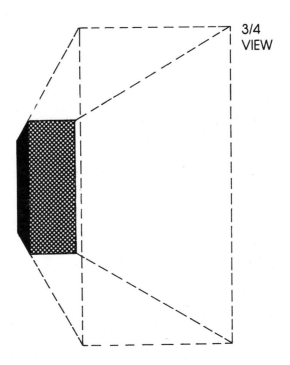

3/4
VIEW

AMPLIFIER

Amplifiers do exactly what the name implies—they provide the power to amplify the sound coming into the microphone and push it through the speakers. Standard amps provide for two or more microphone inputs. If you require more microphones, you will need additional inputs which can be accommodated by a *mixer* (see Example 6).

Ex. 6

Amplifier   Mixer

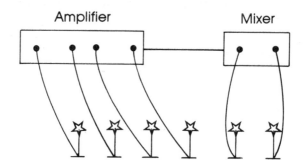

When the rhythm section is added to our original vocal set up, balance becomes not only important to the audience's ears, but to the entire ensemble. The rhythm section must be placed as close together as possible, with eye contact with each other and the conductor a must. The closer the vocal ensemble to the rhythm section, the better for hearing each other and the tighter the ensemble sound.

Ex. 7

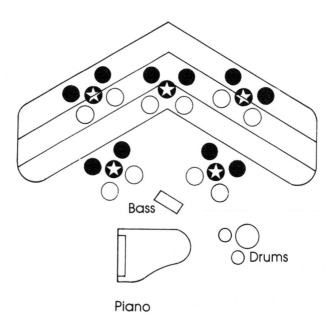

Bass

Drums

Piano

When working with a full stage band, the balance problems will be greatly magnified. As with the rhythm section, placement is critical. In the first example, the voices are on risers behind the stage band. Properly amplified, the voices will carry over the band and the total effect will be sound coming from one point. The danger here is that with the band in front, the voices will have difficulty hearing the instruments. In this set up, proper use of stage monitors (speakers which let the performers hear what is being projected to the audience) is advised.

Ex. 8

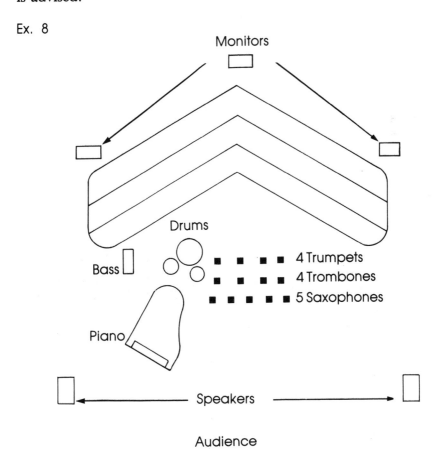

The next example shows the vocal ensemble and the stage band in an inverted "V" formation with the rhythm section in the middle. The problem here would be the same as in the first example—each ensemble would have difficulty hearing each other. By having the rhythm section in the middle, the problem of "time lag" will be reduced.

Ex. 9

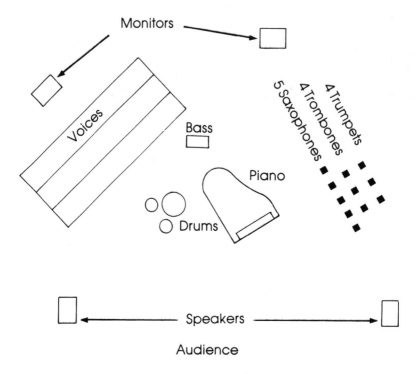

The next example shows the stage band split, with the vocal ensemble in the middle. The benefit here is that the voices are literally surrounded by the sound of the stage band. By having the band separated, the chance of a time lag problem as well as the two sections of the band not hearing each other is greater.

Ex. 10

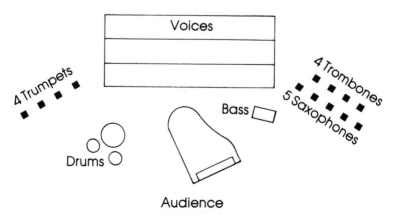

An excellent rehearsal set up is illustrated below. By setting up in a block formation, everyone gets a chance to more clearly hear each other. Since this formation is obviously not appropriate in a concert situation, some directors might feel reluctant to rehearse in one set up and perform in another. When used sparingly, this set up is a valuable rehearsal technique and should be attempted rather than totally disregarded.

Ex. 11

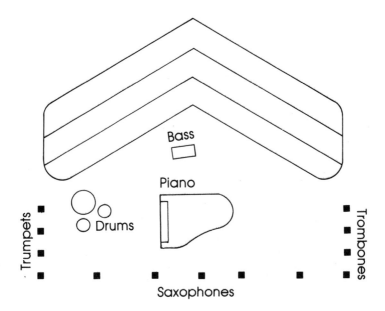

Whatever your choice of vocal–instrumental combination, both physical placement and proper amplification will play an important part in the overall success of the ensemble. Physical placement is largely experimental and the only cost is time and patience. The sound system is another matter. The component parts of an adequate sound system can be very costly, and the decision of what to purchase should be made in consultation with experts in the field. Discuss your needs with your audio-visual department—they will probably have the names of reputable manufacturers, distributors and sound system companies that can help you to design a system to meet your specific requirements.

Chapter Seven
THE
REHEARSAL

A s with any performing group, the key to a successful vocal jazz ensemble will be a well run rehearsal.

A successful rehearsal will have the following components: announcements, the warm up, detail work on performance pieces, some theory and improvisation and sight reading. Since the vocal jazz ensemble will probably be meeting on a less frequent basis than the concert choir, the advance preparation and planning by the director is particularly important.

The rehearsal chart below suggests time slots for the various aspects of the rehearsal. It should only be considered as a guide, and should be tailored to the needs of your particular group.

Ex. 1

Total Rehearsal Time	30 min.	45 min.	60 min.	90 min.
Announcements	1 min.	2 min.	3 min.	4 min.
Warm up	5 min.	8 min.	8 min.	8 min.
Music Practice	15 min.	22 min.	30 min.	50 min.
Theory–Improvisation	5 min.	8 min.	13 min.	15 min.
Sight Reading	4 min.	5 min.	6 min.	13 min.

The announcements should prepare the ensemble for what is expected at each particular rehearsal. The instructions should be clear and concise—"After the warm up, we will work on the blues piece and then start on the new Latin selection. I have selected a new rock piece which we will read and then we will work on some improvisation."

Following the announcements, the warm ups should begin. For the beginning vocal jazz ensemble, warm up exercises are particularly important. The sound and feel of jazz should be ingrained in the ear and mind in preparation for actual performance.

The exercises presented below should act only as a guide to the director. What is important here is that these exercises have been designed to touch on all aspects of the rehearsal and may be used independently as an exercise or in direct conjunction with theory, improvisation and sight reading.

HARMONIC WARM UP

The following exercises present all the triads (major, minor, augmented and diminished), dominant and major sevenths (major and minor), extensions and cluster formations. They should be sung slowly and move chromatically (ascending and descending). The purpose is to develop intonation and a sense of the type of chord being sung. Parts should be interchanged (soprano sing alto, etc.). To further develop the ear, have the singers stand in quartets rather than in sections. The ideal end result of this type of warm up is for the director to play the root and ask the ensemble to build whatever chord he requests. For example, play F, assign an F^9 chord and say "Basses—root, tenors—third, altos—fifth, second sopranos—seventh, first sopranos—ninth."

The combinations of the following chord structures are infinite. The examples below should be treated as a basic outline for all possible inversions, keys and extensions. Be creative!

Ex. 2

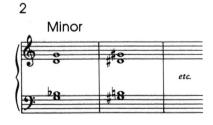

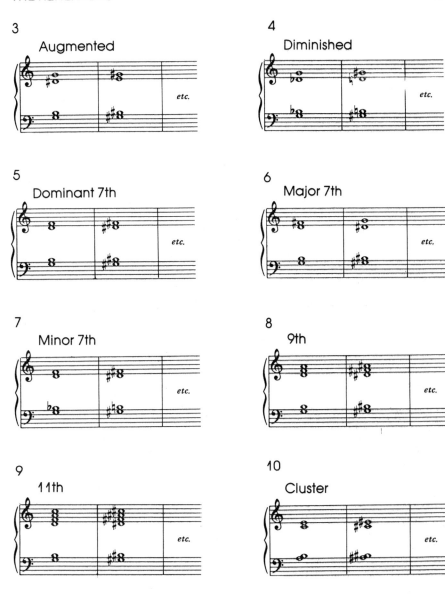

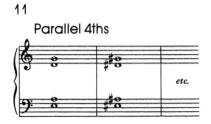

Building further on these rhythmic and melodic responses, our original figure can be developed into a little canon.

Ex. 7

Retaining the original rhythm, we can also alter the "melody" using the same four notes (B, B♭, C, D♭).

Ex. 8

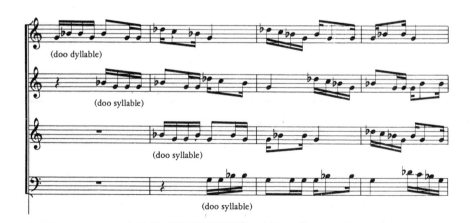

Besides "loosening up" the chorus, these exercises will better prepare the chorus and director in being able to grasp the harmonic and
rhythmic concept of a selection.

Using a passage from *Bright Lights* by Ken Kraintz, application of
these techniques might proceed as follows:

Ex. 9

Clap out the prevailing rhythm:

Ex. 10

Sing the rhythm on one pitch using scat syllables:

Ex. 11

RHYTHMIC AND MELODIC WARM UP

The director or student claps out a rhythm and the ensemble responds likewise. The rhythms should begin simply and increase in length and difficulty. Again the examples below are just examples. The opportunity for creativity here is limitless. All rhythms should be clapped with a jazz feel as well as a rock feel.

Ex. 3

One extension of this exercise is to sing back the rhythm in scat syllables on one pitch. Taking example 4, play or sing the rhythmic figure on G and have the ensemble sing back similarly.

Ex. 4

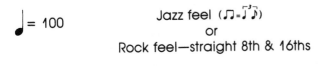

Taking this a step further, play or sing the rhythm on a series of pitches, with the ensemble responding.

Ex. 5

The possibilities can extend to adding harmonies. One effective harmonic device in such an exercise is to sing the line in parallel fourths—all parts then have the "melody."

Ex. 6

Ex. 12

Sing the lyrics in unison (soprano line):

Ex. 13

Explain the function of the chord structure. Minor and major seventh chords moving diatonically—written in simple block form. Sing each chord—move chromatically and then as written below.

Ex. 14

Dm7	Em7	Fmaj7	Em7	Dm7	
					etc.

As you proceed through these exercises and incorporate similar ideas into your performance pieces, the time will come to make the determination as when a selection is ready for public performance. That determination is often subjective, but there are some guidelines to follow.

1. Is the form of the selection clearly understood?
2. Are all the rhythmic patterns being accurately and stylistically sung?
3. Are the themes predominant where they should be, as well as the background voices being soft enough?
4. Is the intonation as precise as possible?
5. Is the rhythm section, or any member of it, too loud or soft?
6. Is the tempo right for this piece?
7. Are the voices articulating identical and similar figures in the same way?
8. Are all the members singing with the same conception and "feel," particularly in the approach to eighth notes?
9. Are the attacks and releases together?
10. Does the drummer fill and kick all the necessary patterns or is he so busy that he has forgotten to lay down solid rhythms?
11. Is each section breathing together—are the words being sung clearly without being stilted or garbled.
12. If your group is involved in improvisation, have the soloists familiarized themselves with the harmonic structure, scales and chord progressions?

Each director will probably find many more questions to ask during the rehearsal. The more questions asked and resolved will ultimately result in a better performance.

The extent and complexity of warm up exercises will depend on the ability and experience of the director and chorus. What is most important is for the ensemble to get the necessary sound and rhythmic pulse in their mind and ear. Anyone can sing a note, push a valve or press a key, but the subtleties of the jazz idiom demand more than that little dot on the printed page. Warm up exercises and rehearsal techniques that include the creative component not only prepare the group musically, but psychologically. For twenty-four voices to execute an ornamentation or inflection as one body requires tremendous discipline, technically and musically, and a complete understanding of the idiom.

Chapter Eight
IMPROVISATION

I f vocalists were as uninhibited about improvising on the stage as they are in the shower or while driving the car (with the windows closed) this chapter might not be necessary. Not that the lack of inhibition makes for great improvisation, but it helps. Improvisation is extemporaneous expression—a variation on a theme performed on the spot. It is not uncontrolled blathering or "doing one's thing," but revolves around form and structure be it a twelve bar blues, the chord progression and/or melodic line of a standard pop tune or within a modal framework.

The element of improvisation was a natural state of the art among jazz players and vocalists simply because they could not read music and had little or no formal training. They depended solely on their ear and whatever technique they developed on their own. The art of jazz was learned "on the streets" and the aspiring jazz performer had to immerse himself in the often ruthless arena of the jam session to get his education.

When the sounds of jazz were put on paper (usually for big band arrangements) and the improvised variations became more complex, the study of jazz, out of necessity, became more formalized and academic. Today, the great young jazz artists are, for the most part, university educated and display remarkable technical and creative facility. But despite what "technical" advances might have been developed during the span of jazz history, there is a common bond that defies technique and training and that is the feel of the music—something that is immediately understood and recognized by performers and fans of the art.

The mystery surrounding jazz and its improvisational quality has slowly disappeared as its availability and popularity has increased. Not only is jazz thriving in its purest forms, but it has managed to infiltrate its stylizations into many forms of more commercially acceptable popular music.

What does this all mean for the choral director who has to prepare for the Spring concert, buck awkward schedules or worry if the accompanist will show for rehearsal?

"Who has time for improvisation—besides, what will the parents say when their child who takes private lessons every Saturday morning at twenty bucks a throw steps up to the microphone and sings "sha-ba-da-bop."

The only humane reply is to refer back to our cousin the stage band and realize the growing pains he had to endure, and the fact that the band director applying for a high school position had better be able to handle a stage band and have a respectable background in jazz or he very well might not get the job. The stage band is well entrenched and a solid part of the instrumental curriculum, and from all indications, the jazz vocal ensemble and its swing and show choir counterparts are moving in the same direction.

There is a wealth of material available on the techniques of jazz improvisation. Although most of the methods in print today are geared to the instrumentalist, they are, in theory, applicable to the vocalist. (See Materials Guide.)

The best teacher of improvisation is the ear. There is no substitute for listening, and all the theory books dealing with improvisation are absolutely useless unless one is prepared to take the time to train his ears.

Rather than dealing in theoretical concepts, this chapter will present examples of transcribed solos with the original melodic line and harmonic progressions. All of these transcriptions were taped in workshop and clinic situations with soloists being students and teachers.

Since the first selection, *A Little Bit of Love*, Example 1, is not written in a jazz style, it was a bit surprising that the young lady who wanted to do so sang such an interesting solo. What is interesting about this particular solo is that she used the melodic line rather than the chord progression as the basis for her improvisation. She stays quite close to the original line and makes use of both the lyric and scat syllables. By what she does at measure 17 and 18 she probably has done some extensive listening. Those two measures illustrate a highly stylized "bop" line in the way she accents the after beats and the fact that she hears the flat 9 (D♭) of the chord. Measures 23, 24, 25, and 26 present a tricky progression (especially the Bm^7 to G♯m^7) so she shows a healthy sense of caution and holds the common tone of B rather than trying to move linearly through this harmonic sequence.

Ex. 1

A LITTLE BIT OF LOVE

Earlier in this chapter, it was mentioned that the aspiring young jazz musician had to place himself in the "ruthless arena of the jam session." If you also remember, the chapter on harmony discussed the almost infinite variations on the blues progression. One of the "tests of manhood" in the jam session was for the piano player to arbitrarily alter the harmonic progression of the blues during the course of the singers or horn players solo. The soloists acceptance (or nonacceptance) into the group depended how well (or poorly) he managed to play on whatever progression or variation he was presented with. I relate this situation because of the circumstances surrounding the next example. The clinic dealt with vocal improvisation of the blues. A volunteer chorus assembled on the stage and they were asked to sing and repeat the unison line (as illustrated) while various soloists attempted to improvise on the basic I—IV—V^7 blues progression. (See Chapter Two, Example 11.) Well into the eighth chorus, a young man stepped up to the microphone and within two measures, the members of the rhythm section realized that this fellow knew exactly what he was doing. When the second chorus came around, the rhythm section shifted gears and presented our remarkable soloist with a variation of the blues progression that can unnerve all but the best. Well, "superear," as we later called him, sang the solo you see below. Remember, he had to anticipate where the progression was going and respond vocally—on the spot! The sequential figures in measures 7, 8 and 9 are particularly impressive both in concept and execution. By way of his scat syllables, we appropriately entitled his solo "Ch' Goo Bee Doo Yah Wah."

Ex. 2

♩ = 120

(Jazz feel)

doo n doo n doo____ sha bah dah dah doo____

Cm7(sus4)   B7♭5   B♭9   B♭m7   E♭7

4   5   6

sha bah doo wee doo wah__ I   like to sing the blues,__   like to sing the blues.___

Am7   D7   A♭m7   D♭7   Gm7

7   8   9

doo n doo sha bah dah wah__   wah   ooo shoo doo n   doo

C11   Am7(13)   D7#9   G7   C9   F6

10   11   12

Most any selection can be opened for improvisation. In fact, there is really not such a thing as a "jazz" tune; only songs that lay well for improvisation. (In the trade, there are "good tunes" and "bad tunes"—good tunes have "nice" changes and lines, bad tunes don't—simple as that.)

Aside from the blues and "Rhythm" changes, jazz performers for years have recognized the wealth of material produced by Berlin, Gershwin, Rogers, Hart & Hammerstein, Kurt Weill and most recently, the Beatles. Their compositions were not intended to be "jazz" tunes, but the harmonic, linear and lyrical richness of these songs have always been a natural format for improvisation. (They are "good tunes.") A popular composer that contradicts this situation is Burt Bacharach. A superb writer, his distinctive compositions defy improvisation. They are so thoroughly written and complete that to improvise on such a finished product will sound ludicrous.

The next example, *Mistletoe and Love*, is a Christmas song. Although it is by no means a jazz selection, a teacher felt moved enough to sing a line above the written choral arrangement. It is a simple line, but very effective and within the mood of the piece.

Ex. 3

MISTLETOE AND LOVE

As was mentioned in an earlier chapter, stylized jazz lines are often written into vocal and instrumental parts as a guide for the student. Usually, the chord changes as well as the written piano part are printed to further assist the singer.

   In the next example, *Wind of Life,* a written jazz line is provided in
the piano part at letter D. The chorus sets up the chord pattern while
the improvised or written solo is being played. At this particular
reading session, four vocalists stepped up to the microphone and read
the piano line using scat syllables. (They had obviously rehearsed.)
Reading the written line can be very effective, but what usually happens as the line is practiced, is that the singer begins to add his own
inflections and restructures the line and the process of creative improvisation begins to take shape.

Ex. 4

= 120

Bossa Nova   WIND OF LIFE

Although there are professional jazz singers who are able to success-fully sing in an instrumental style, particularly at fast tempos (hard running and syncopated eighth note figures using scat syllables), it should be stressed that this is a musical and vocal skill of the first order. Most student vocalists, with few exceptions, have neither the ability nor the musical maturity to successfully manage such complex improvisations.

The process of learning the art of improvisation takes time and patience for the student and the director. Don't jump into material that is beyond the capabilities of your ensemble or put your students in the position of attempting jazz solos that are not natural to his or her own musical style and development. The beauty of the voice is in the advantage it has over the instrument—the lyric. A well-written lyric and melodic line combined with a singer who has a sense of phrasing cannot be duplicated instrumentally. Develop the singer who is able to make tasteful embellishments within a lyrical ballad. If the interest is there and the student listens to the pros, his or her abilities will develop to the point where faster tempos and possibly scat chorus' will be a natural part of the improvisational process. Remember that hard is not better—good singing is. And improvisa-tion can be outstanding when it is personal and spontaneous and not forced.

Chapter Nine

PUBLISHERS, COMPOSERS/ARRANGERS AND YOU

U nless the music educator is fortunate enough to have access to tailor-made arrangements, he will be using music produced by the educational publishers. A testament to the publishers efforts is reflected in the amount of promotional materials, recordings and other assorted information sitting on countless desks (or wastepaper baskets) waiting to be studied. And the amount of material increases, making the job of perusal more time consuming and difficult. Not only have established publishers been printing more music, but new companies have been sprouting up like mushrooms in a wet cave, each trying to provide the music teacher with the best possible product.

Decisions of what to print is a carefully thought out process and depends to a great extent on feedback from teachers at conventions, clinics, reading sessions and from the vast chain of music distributors across the country.

Along with such concrete information, the publisher must also have a certain intuitive sense of what the "market" is all about. After all, the educator and the publisher share the same concern—quality material that makes musical and educational sense.

The interest in pop and jazz oriented music has, to a great extent, contributed to the enormous amount of music printed every year for school use. Aside from "original" material (music composed specifically for the educational publisher) some publishers have access to the vast amount of music produced and recorded for the "commercial" market. Under certain circumstances, the publisher can license, rearrange and distribute this type of music for a variety of instrumental and vocal settings. Licensing agreements can vary in complexity but basically it means that the educational publisher has permission from the copyright holder to make the selection suitable for school use.

Another area of availability is music that periodically enters into the "public domain." Every year copyrights expire, thereby releasing a piece of music from any legal restrictions. When a selection enters into public domain, only the specific arrangement or edition is subject to copyright, leaving the composition free for anyone to publish.

So with the combination of original, licensed and public domain, coupled with substantial demand, the amount of music available to the educator has grown rapidly.

But availability does not always mean practicality—practical in the sense that any selection is suitable for school use. For example, how sensible are the lyrics? The melodic line and the potential for an interesting arrangement might be present, but does it make sense to publish a piece where the lyrics might be objectionable? What about the magic of the recording studio? Is it reasonable to publish a "Top 40" piece that depends so heavily on highly sophisticated recording techniques that no amount of arranging can duplicate the recording? "It doesn't sound like the original." Of course not—where are the overdubbed strings, the reverb, the multi-tracked voices and the ten man rhythm section? Will the school have a decent rhythm section? Certain selections will fall flat unless an adequate rhythm section is supporting the voices, particularly selections that require a "heavy rock feel." The basic question is really whether a piece of music can stand on its own.

When the issue of availability and practicality are resolved, the publisher must then decide on an arranger. And in an area of such varying student abilities and combinations, vocal and instrumental, the choice of arrangers becomes crucial to the success of the piece.

The limitations placed on the arranger writing for very specific types of performing groups (changing voice, mens chorus, womens chorus, chorus with stage band, elementary band, etc.) and styles of music (secular, jazz, pop, etc.) are enormous, and it takes skill and creativity to allow these restrictions to work and be musical.

Although some publishing companies employ full time staff arrangers, most contract writers on a free lance basis. The composer/arranger may be identified with one publisher (by choice or contract) or may write for a number of publishers. Generally, writers work on a fee schedule (per arrangement), a royalty (percentage of sales) or a combination of both. The illegal and fraudulent nature of copying music may best be understood when one realizes the cost to the publisher of production, advertising and printing, plus the fact that fees and royalties may represent a substantial portion of the writers income.

Based on all the information gathered by the publisher and the arranger, the decision to publish or not is determined. The process then includes the actual arranging of the piece, a series of proofreadings by the editor, arranger and possibly an outside proofreader and then to print, promotion and hopefully and eventually to the teacher. The time elapsed varies, but generally the process takes about six months.

The teacher is now faced with all that promotional material on his desk. More than often, and rather than spending the time, the teacher will rely on past successful experiences. "What does publisher X have" or "is there anything new by composer so and so," or recommendations from fellow directors.

This might be the most expedient method of adding music to the teachers library, but by doing so, the teacher is denying himself the opportunity to discover the full range of new material. Probably the best way to become acquainted with new music is to attend clinics and reading sessions sponsored by music dealers and publishers.

After all the advertising, reading sessions, clinics and discussions with colleagues, some teachers will have the thought that perhaps they might "do it better," and toy with the idea of submitting a selection for publication. Why not? The chances are that there are many fine composers and arrangers lurking in the background. But how does one go about getting a piece published? If the thought has crossed your mind, you have probably done some writing for your group, discovered that it sounds pretty good and based on what you have seen and heard in print, feel that your music at least deserves a chance.

What are the obstacles? First and foremost, publishers tend to go with writers of proven success, so as an unknown quantity, you will have to present yourself and your music in the best possible light. Provide a neat and complete manuscript. A lead line with lyrics and chord changes is usually not acceptable. Enclose a cassette or tape of your piece along with a cover letter indicating why you feel your piece has merit—musically and educationally. A preliminary phone call to the editor can be helpful and will prepare him for your package. Do not send an arrangement of a copyrighted selection (a current pop tune, for example) unless you are sure that the publisher holds the copyright. Licensing of music is the publishers decision, not the writers, and the chances of evaluating a selection that the publisher cannot easily acquire is quite slim. Know the publisher—don't send a jazz piece to a publisher who specializes in religious music. Also, there is no need to file for copyright. Well known publishers with established reputations are quite forthright and honest and are not in the business to "steal" music.

Once your music has been submitted, be patient—it takes time to study a score and there are probably many other packages like yours waiting to be evaluated. If your piece is rejected, despair not. Surprisingly, rejections are not always based on musical decisions. Your piece might not fit into the present production schedule (such schedules are often determined a year or more in advance). It may be stylistically removed from what the publisher has decided to release (again, know your publisher). In most cases, the publisher will provide a reasonable explanation for his decision. Your recourse at this point is to try another publisher—and don't give up, especially if you feel that your piece has merit.

If your composition or arrangement is accepted for publication, you will enter into a contract that assigns the copyright to the publisher. Legally, the publisher will "own" the piece and will absorb all expenses related to publication (printing, promotion, distribution, etc.). In exchange, the composer will be entitled to a royalty (if an "original") of usually 10 percent of the retail price of the total copies sold and paid for. Now that you are a full fledged composer, don't expect to become rich! The educational music world is not the commercial "pop" market. Although there are financial benefits, the real reward is the thought that somewhere out there, there are a group of musicians performing and enjoying your contribution and creation.

The field of educational publishing can be complex, at times risky and is geared 100 percent to the needs and efforts of the music educator. Each publisher has a "style" or "tone" that is distinctive and may be reflected in its printing process, the type and quality of its music, its clinicians and personnel.

Of course no one publisher can satisfy the requirements of every director of a performing group, so the competition among publishers to capture your interest has created quality as well as quantity and will continue to do so. Your response to what they print plays a great part in what will be included in future publications. This response is not only reflected in what music you purchase, but the communication you have (or should have) with the publisher. This is a very special relationship and one that should be nurtured and developed. Write to the publisher—compliments, complaints and suggestions are all welcome. Have you recently performed a piece that you particularly like? Drop the composer a note in care of the publisher telling him so. You will probably receive a letter in return with a hearty "thank you." Did you find a printing mistake in a recently purchased octavo—let the publisher know. It will probably be corrected in the next printing.

Keep the lines of communication open. Since your reactions and responses are so important to publishers, you should not hesitate to be a part of the publishing process and provide the necessary feedback that will continue to improve and insure the quality of music you and future generations of choral directors will perform.

"THE BEST EXAMPLES OF WHAT TO DO ARE BY THOSE WHO DO IT BEST"

With this quote in mind, I felt the inclusion of the following two articles would be very interesting and informative to everyone interested in this book.

The first article, *Perfectionist Carmen McRae* by Harvey Siders gives us insight to the solo jazz vocalist. The second, *The Backup Singers: High Reward for a Privileged Few* by Don Heckman approaches the "behind the scene" vocal specialists in todays recording industry.

HARVEY SIDERS is currently with ABC–TV News in Los Angeles as a newswriter and producer of documentaries. Formerly the West Coast editor for **Down Beat Magazine**, he has written for **Life, Saturday Review, Coronet, The Boston Globe, San Francisco Chronicle, BMI Magazine, International Musician, Different Drummer, Guitar Player, Contemporary Keyboard,** and **Jazz Magazine.** He continues to contribute to the **Los Angeles Examiner, Radio Free Jazz** and reviews music for the **Los Angeles Times** and the **San Fernando Valley News.** While attending Berklee and Boston University, he led his own jazz trio. Mr. Siders is on the adjunct faculty of USC's School of Journalism where he teaches newswriting. The following article was written for the 1978 Fall issue of **Jazz Magazine.** Used by permission of the author and publisher.

PERFECTIONIST CARMEN McRAE

by Harvey Siders

There are stares, there are glares. There are looks that kill, looks that chill. And then, there is that non pareil: the frenetic, splenetic scowl of Carmen McRae. Hell hath no fury like Carmen betrayed by a back-up musician.

Ella gets out there and just swings, Sarah Vaughn runs a gamut from divine to sassy. Ah, but Carmen. I've seen her reduce sidemen to a pile of dust with her laser beam reactions, then turn around and inform her patrons that someone in the backfield blew the play. I've squirmed for the guilty party, but at the same time I've secretly applauded the quest for perfection that separates Carmen from the other living legends in that exclusive first-name club of jazz singers.

Jazz singers like Carmen, Ella and Sarah are an endangered species today. If they don't preserve their art and maintain the high standards that are synonymous with that triumvirate, they won't last long enough to spawn the next generation of jazz vocalists.

No one, but no one, works harder at perfecting or protecting her talents than Carmen McRae. She picks the material, sets the tempo, and has every right to expect the correct changes and voicings behind her so she can concentrate on the lyrics and shape her unique phrasing that has made her the only singer in captivity who can belt them out in italics. When she underlines *Guess Who I Saw Today My Dear* she's selling a potent piece of melodrama, and she shouldn't have to worry about being harmonically detoured by someone behind her.

It's the listeners that count, Carmen explained: "If they hear me go off, or if they hear something go wrong, they're not going to blame one of those cats back there. They're going to blame me! That's what it all stems from. I don't enjoy embarrassing a musician. I really don't enjoy doing that. But I concentrate very hard on what I'm doing up there, and so should they. They're getting paid very good money for what they're doing. There's no reason why they can't get it right—especially since we rehearse everything to death."

I recalled one recent incident at the Playboy Club in Los Angeles when the poor bass player felt like digging a hole for himself. After the set I tried to talk to the trio, but I arrived just as someone else did with the nullifying message, "Miss McRae wants to see the musicians in the dressing room." Now that's the true meaning of a "command performance." All three headed for the confrontation as if they were walking that proverbial last mile.

When I mentioned that to Carmen, she replied, "Well, when something like that happens, I call them in and say, 'You're playing bad tonight. What's going on.?' And I remind them, 'Look, if I do something wrong, I'll get out of it somehow. If you do something wrong, I don't know where I'm at. So concentrate. I don't intend to do another show like that!'

"And another thing. You know, musicians voice chords differently all the time. A B-flat 9th to you may come out different to someone else. Now if we're doing a tune and at a certain crucial point I need a chord in a particular way to get into another tune, and Marshal (pianist Marshal Otwell) has changed it, I'm standing there with egg on my face and I say to Marshal 'I don't get it. What's that supposed to be?' Then he plays it right and I'll say, 'Thank you very much.'

"People don't realize what goes on sometimes behind the scenes. But I know this much: I'm not paying them to make me look like an idiot. I pay them to make me look good."

Let there be no doubt: Most of the time her musicians make Carmen look great. She may win through intimidation on occasion, but for the most part she wins through expertise. She sets one hell of an example for her sidemen and they almost invariably rise to the occasion.

Carmen has been rising to the occasion now for more than three decades, starting in the forties with the bands of Benny Carter, Count Basie and Mercer Ellington, then paying her solo dues at Minton's as a singer and intermission pianist. By the early fifties she began her long odyssey from one label to another: Stardust, Venus, Decca, Kapp, Columbia, Mainstream, Bethlehem, Atlantic and Blue Note. She's finally got an exclusive deal now, with Universal, and this Fall she'll know whether she's finally found a home.

Meanwhile she's at home in just about any type of club setting, from rooms considered part of the "chitlin circuit" to the most posh, antiseptic bistros. She can size up an audience at the drop of a down beat and adjust her material and chatter accordingly.

"But no matter what songs I sing, the lyrics have to be meaningful and believable—unless, of course, you're doing uptempo tunes. Then nobody listens to the words. They're too busy keeping time to the rhythm. The songs being written today seems to have no lasting value to them. There are a few, of course, that may be around for a while, but the only contemporary tunes that stand a chance of becoming standards are the Beatle tunes.

"I like songs of love and life, and I like tunes that have pretty verses to them. They're not writing verses anymore and that's a shame. I especially like to do well-known standards that have unfamiliar verses. Take *Stardust*, for example. Everyone knows the verse to that one. But on something like *My Funny Valentine*, no one knows the verse, so when you finish it and up comes a familiar chorus, everyone reacts to that."

Everyone reacts to certain tunes that Carmen is known for and they constantly request them; *Alfie, For Once in My Life, Drunk in San Francisco*, and especially *Guess Who I Saw Today*. That latter tune is given such a unique reading, no one else should dare sing it. The song is so closely identified with Carmen that she "owns" it.

"Well I was the first to record that, you know, and I made some changes in it—with the permission of the writer, of course—so whenever I hear someone else sing it the way I do, I know they've only heard my version. Anyway, that's one of the tunes I keep on the side. (The aforementioned requests) They're not part of my regular show."

As mentioned, her regular show varies according to geography and mood. I've seen her devote an entire set to the old standards; and I've seen her accent the contemporary. I remember one show dominated by deliciously dirty blues; other times she gets the urge to clear the stand and accompany herself. That's when the audience accompanies Carmen on a trip back to Minton's—to a less complicated time when all we had to worry about was a world war.

Her piano playing reveals formal training. It's correct, yet imaginative. So of course I was interested in hearing her selection of the "ideal trio." In other words, who would she take with her for a "Fantasy Island" gig?

"Well on piano, my favorites are George Shearing or Oscar Peterson. I say 'or' because it's not necessarily in that order. On bass there is only one. No choice. Andy Simpkins, period. And I'd like Harvey Mason on drums, or Joey Baron, who I have used."

She had a spectacular combo recently for a memorable concert that is now available on Blue Note, "Live At the Hollywood Bowl: The Los Angeles Philharmonic Orchestra." That night is indelibly etched in my memory because Sarah Vaughn shared the stage with Carmen. It was, in the old fashioned sense of the phrase, a cutting contest, like the vintage jam sessions in which instrumentalists would sit in and try to outdo each other.

To be fair, as well as accurate, the only winner was the audience (the Bowl holds in excess of 17,000). It was a grand night for swinging and Carmen looks back on it fondly. "Now ordinarily I prefer to hear just a basic trio behind me. That provides the ultimate freedom for me. But when I heard that symphony orchestra that night—I don't know how many there are in it, 100 or so?—oh Lord, what a sound! And not only that, but—the charts were by Bill Holman. What more need I say?"

Well she could have said more about her checkered recording career. Most critics, and most of her adoring fans will agree that she hasn't been done justice by her producers, engineers and above all, those in charge of promotion. A typical excerpt from our conversation seemed to sum up the frustration she manages to control with her sardonic sense of humor.

"Are you satisfied with anything you've recorded?"

"There must be something I'm satisfied with. Somewhere along the line."

"What do you think is the best thing you've done on disc?"

"I ain't made it yet!"

Pity. Someone like Carmen McRae should have a dozen albums she could pick at random and point to with pride. However, musicians are constantly pointing with pride at Carmen. She likes to drop into the local jazz joints—unobtrusively, if possible—and dig the scene. But anonymity eludes her the way chartbound albums elude her. "I resent it when musicians feel obligated to make a big thing of my being in a club and calling me up to perform. Now don't get me wrong: I love to sit in, but I'd rather be in the mood to do it. I'd much rather go over to the piano player and ask him if he feels like having me do a couple of tunes.

"One danger for me when it comes to sitting in is that I can never think of what tunes to do. Worse yet, I constantly forget what key I do most of my tunes in. I'll never forget one time—I don't remember what club it was—I gave the piano player the wrong key. Well I never did sing the melody. Man, I was so far away from it I had to improvise the entire song!"

It's safe to say the patrons got their money's worth that night. Carmen never disappoints. Perhaps that's what separates the girls from the women. Carmen is such a poised, polished confident pro, she can do no wrong. If she says she "had to improvise," rest assured she did just that: improvise, not fake. There's quite a difference.

In connection with that, I asked her if her italicized phrasing is entirely her own doing, or had she been influenced by some earlier stylists. "I swear I don't know where it came from. I know I never copied anyone else. It just happened, that's all." She claims her manner of phrasing crystallized during that period when she was accompanying herself at Minton's. If there's any correlation between singing and talking, then it's obvious Carmen came by her particular style completely naturally. Her conversation is liberally sprinkled with italics. She constantly stresses certain points much the way Pearl Bailey brings out words in bold relief. It's colorful, lively, dramatic, filled with humor and pathos, and rivets your attention. All of which neatly sums up Carmen's vocalizing.

With her unique phrasing, she neatly summed up the state of the music business today, especially in connection with the plight of young singers. But of course the printed word can't capture the flavor of her interjections. In essence, however, she had this to say: "There's plenty of work out there—at least for the established singers. Ella, Sarah, Peggy Lee, Mel Torme, Joe Williams are working all the time. And I certainly can't complain. There's a lot of work for name singers. But I'm pessimistic about the outlet for those who need it: the young unknown singers. Where are they going to learn their craft? Where are they going to pay their dues? I'm also pessimistic about the future of jazz singing. That is jazz singing as we know it. It's a disappearing art. The young, upcoming singers aren't singing pure jazz. At least I don't hear them."

I was curious to find out what went through her mind when she's singing. It turned out to be only one thing, and that should come to no surprise to any of her fans—lyrics. Words are her lifeblood, and no matter how fast or slow, raucous or rock-ish, sensitive or sensous the tune may be, Carmen is well aware that the message is the medium.

One medium that really turns Carmen these days—or nights—is disco. Not so much as a participant, but as a connoisseur of body language. "I love anything that makes you want to get up and shake all over. So it's not confined to disco. I dig bossa nova. When you hear a good jazz samba, you just gotta get up and move something."

Hearing that come from Carmen McRae. I couldn't help thinking that she is one of the few jazz flavored singers who can make a ballad a real moving experience. What she said about concentrating on lyrics is actually an understatement. She is a study in intensity, regardless of how relaxed she appears to be on the stand. And the intensity, as we have already learned, extends to the quality of her accompaniment.

It seems to underscore an insightful remark she made regarding one of her early idols, Billie Holiday. It was quoted by Dan Morgenstern in his book, "Jazz People": "The only time Billie is at ease and at rest with herself is when she sings." Paradoxically, that seems to be in direct conflict with Carmen's own personality. She happens to be one of the most charming, down to earth persons I know in the business. Carmen's uninhibited laughter can fill a room, and it often fills Dodger Stadium. She's one of the home teams's funkiest fans.

Asked about personal goals, Carmen returned to the subject of recordings, and her new contract with Universal Records. "I'm optimistic, yet I really must withhold judgment until that first release comes out." She's going to record in New York, but she's not going to take her regular trio with her. "I'm going to leave that aspect of the session entirely in their hands. But as far as something else is concerned, I've already laid down the law. I've told them I want a hit record out of this deal. I want a single that makes the charts. 'Cause I'm tired of working so damn hard. I want to be able to pick and choose my gigs. And if I get me a record that makes that kind of noise, I just might be able to do just that."

Here's hoping she makes a most joyful noise.

* * *

DON HECKMAN is currently a freelance television screenwriter and lives in the Los Angeles area. Trained as a musician, Mr. Heckman received his B.A. in Theory from Florida State and his M.A. in Musicology from the City College of New York where he taught a number of jazz related courses. Before moving to California, Mr. Heckman was the East Coast Vice-President for A & R at RCA, and the Daily Rock and Pop critic and the Sunday Edition Recordings editor for **The New York Times.** His many writing credits include articles for the **Village Voice, Stereo Review, Downbeat, Metronome** and **Jazz Magazine.** The following article appeared in the 1978 September issue of **High Fidelity Magazine.** Used by permission of the author and publisher

THE BACKUP SINGERS:
HIGH REWARD FOR A PRIVILEGED FEW

by Don Heckman

Their names are not the stuff of which legends are made, even if some—Cher, Rita Coolidge, and Pattie Brooks—have moved on to bigger and better things. But most—like Brooks Hunnicutt, Jim Gilstrap, Shirley Matthews, and Becky Lopez—are perhaps familiar in name, but only through vague recollection of small print credits on the backs of innumerable albums. Most of them we know not as names at all, but as voices whose insistence that "you deserve a break today," or "you asked for it, you've got it," resounds in our subconscious long after we've forgotten the products they sing about.

Who are they? The background singers. Or, to use some of the terms that they themselves prefer, the studio singers, the session singers, or the group singers. These are the performers who very often make the difference between just another record and a "Top 10" hit; they are the musical mouthpieces for virtually every company that advertises on radio and television; and, sometimes, they are the lyrical voices we hear issuing from such "singing" movie actors as Elizabeth Taylor, Jennifer O'Neill, and the late Peter Finch.

"We give them whatever they want," says Matthews, a thirteen-year veteran of Los Angeles recording studios. "Country, legit, down-home, funky—we do it." Matthews has backed artists ranging from Linda Ronstadt, Barbra Streisand, and Neil Sedaka to Steely Dan and the Doobie Brothers, and is one of fifty to sixty singers in the Los Angeles chapter of the American Federation of Television and Radio Artists (AFTRA) who make a full time living from studio work.

Matthews has two prime areas of activity—records and commercial spots. The female trio she prefers to work with can always produce the most popular current "sound" for vocal backup groups. "The style today is the black sound," says AFTRA recording representative Albert Moore, a former lead singer with the folk/rock group, Sweetwater. "The influence of three-voice black female trios is pervasive. More recently, since the great success of the Bee Gee's disco-style recordings, there seems to be a resurgence of white male ensemble styles. But it could change again next week. It all goes in cycles."

No matter how much the styles change, singers like Matthews, Vanetta Fields, and Gilstrap will provide whatever the producers need. They're prepared to be flexible, and they're used to being simply another element in the production process. As Fields puts it: "You don't talk back, and you don't talk out of turn. You're there to listen and do you're part. That's what it's all about."

Session work falls into two broad catagories: head dates and chart dates. In the former, the arrangements are worked out on the spot (in the head) during the session usually by the singers working in association with the producer. For the latter, charts—or arrangements—are written out beforehand by the arranger. For Matthews, the split between the two is fairly even: "This week it was a head date, and a good one, for Linda Ronstadt. Next week it'll be charts for Neil Sedaka—and his are always well written."

Many of the younger singers, especially those who have come into the business without formal training, prefer head dates. The spontaneous working out of background riffs, counterlines, etc., is an easy step or two away from the way they worked with the rock groups and vocal ensembles in which many of them began. Some of the older, more traditionally trained singers have mixed emotions about head sessions and the performers who specialize in them. "A lot of performers these days are good rote singers," one oldtimer told me. "They sing well on head charts, they have the right feeling for contemporary rock, but their careers are extremely limited because they simply don't have the technical expertise—the reading ability and the wide range of musical understanding that's needed to cover the kind of music that's thrown at you over the course of let's say a ten-, fifteen-, or twenty-year career in the studios."

Others are more positive about the semi-improvisational sessions. "Sure," says one, "head dates can be a drag to those of us who have the skills and the experience to read anything they put in front of us. But the fact is that they're more creative—it makes us feel as though we're more a part of things."

Creative though they may be, head dates pay not a penny more—or less—than chart dates. The national AFTRA scale for group singers is $35.50 per hour or per record side, with a minimum call of two hours. Solos and duos get $90 per hour, and of course there are some singers who are able to demand double time rates. Except for a minimal royalty rate (similar to that for session instrumentalists) from record sales, the payments stop right there. Virtually every session singer and player in the business complains about the inequity of this arrangement, but they do not seem to have the clout to do much about it.

"The royalty is so small it's practically nonexistent," says one singer. "I know a girl who sang on a Seals and Croft No. 1 record and got something like a $70 royalty payment for it. She was so insulted she framed the check and hung it on the wall!"

There are no such complaints about jingle sessions. Here the residual payment system works so well that it has put a few Los Angeles commercial singers into the highest income tax brackets. Though scale is basically the same as for record dates, jingles can yield as much as $10,000 a year in residuals. Payment depends on how the spot is aired. For "wild" spots—those that appear only in local programming areas—the singer earns a set fee, and the commercial can be used on an unlimited basis for a thirteen-week period. The more lucrative are the "A" spots, which appear on network television during prime time. For these, a residual is earned every time the spot is used.

Obviously, the potential is enormous, though singers can never be sure in advance whether the spot they're doing will run "wild" for a few months or for years in network prime time. "It's all a crap shoot," says Stan Farber. "You never know if the spot you've done will pay straight scale or $10,000 the next year."

Farber has been a studio singer for years, ever since he and Ron Hicklin—perhaps the West Coast's most successful session vocalist—left the state of Washington and moved south to seek their musical fortunes in Glittertown. Farber went through the pop recording mills in the sixties, providing backups for everyone from the Monkees and the Partridge Family to Hugo Montenegro. Now he is the president of the L.A. Chapter of AFTRA and one of the town's active commercial singers. "I couldn't have gotten into it without a solid musical background," he says. "Jingle singers have to have very specific skills. We have to be able to blend—and blend well—with each other, be in tune, sing much more complex harmonies (with closer intervals than you hear in most pop recordings), and deal with more complex rhythms. Maybe most important of all, we have to have good diction. The agency guys want to understand every word we sing—and it's not hard to guess why."

With the stakes so high, it's understandable that producers and contractors are apt to hire the same few singers for the best jingle gigs. So a successful commercial singer's yearly income range is probably between $40,000 and $200,000—or more. In New York, there are probably six performers in the very top brackets (around a quarter of a million dollars a year). In Los Angeles there are probably no more than two. Three or four hover around the $100,000 mark, eight or ten between $50,000 and $100,000, and the rest under $40,000. The bulk of the commercial recording activity takes place in New York, with Los Angeles and Chicago second and third, respectively. Therefore, although a New York perfomer can make his or her income doing jingle dates alone, an L.A. singer who reaches the $200,000 level does everything—jingles, records, film soundtracks, and television. Ron Hicklin's credits range from *Butch Cassidy and the Sundance Kid* and background music for *Happy Days* and *Laverne and Shirley* to some two hundred records that went to the "Top 10," 135 movies, and commercial dates for almost everybody (including Honda, Suzuki, Yamaha and Kawasaki).

Hicklin also works as a contractor. Contracting for studio singers is always done by one of the performers—unlike instrumentalist's sessions where it is frequently handled by a nonperforming musician. The system has its good and bad aspects. Understandably, it helps contribute to the perpetuation of cliques that dominate most of the work. On the other hand, it places more responsibility on the contractor to hire people who work well and effectively with each other, since he himself will be working with them.

"You can bet that when I work as a contractor I'm listening a lot more carefully to things than I did when I was simply one of the hired hands," Hicklin says. "I want to know what the people I'm working with can do—what I can expect from them, without embarrassing them or embarrassing me. I also want to know what they can't do."

Hicklin is, to use his term, almost "paranoid" about wanting to be judged purely on the basis of his singing. He habitually turns down dates on which singers are also asked to be "spear carriers," to serve as extras for the party sequences of TV variety shows, etc. "I'm a singer, not an entertainer," he says, "and that's what I look for in the singers I hire. I try to find people who sing well in tune, who have good rhythm, who read extremely well, who have excellent articulation of lyrics. When a vocal group really nails the rhythm and the words down together, when nothing is mushy or indistinct, it's really an impressive thing to hear."

Unlike Hicklin, many singers have found the self-effacing life as a background singer tough to deal with. Most started out with the idea of being soloists—perhaps of being stars—and few have found it easy to abandon these ambitions. Soprano Sally Stevens has been the National Academy of Arts & Sciences' (NARAS) "Most Valuable Backup Singer" for four years and is a regular on the Burt Bacharach tours. Yet, though she is one of the West Coast's busiest—and wealthiest—commercial artists, she has had moments of real despair about her career. "I went through a period once," she says, "in which I practically resented what I was doing because it was so impersonal and so restricting insofar as any individual self-expression was concerned. What saved it for me was my own writing and my own live performing of things that were mine."

"I'm just thankful," she says, "for the chance to do things just for the sake of doing them." Her most recent art-for sanity's sake outing was a remarkable performance of Luciano's Berio's *Folk Songs*.

Despite it all, most background singers are eminently happy with what they are doing. "Look," says Farber, "how can you complain about being paid well for doing interesting work? Sure, producers tend to overcategorize people: They want a good black lead singer, they get Jim Gilstrap; they want a good bass, they get Gene Morford; they want a high girl who can sound white or black, they hire Carolyn Willis, who can sing anything." But most of us have a pretty big creative share in almost anything we do. The days where vocal performers simply came in like sheep, read the music and went home, are long gone.

It's a safe bet that the good group singers—the ones who are versatile enough to do all the different styles that are called for, from head dates to the most complex chart reading sessions will have longer, more fruitful careers than almost any performer whose single-minded goal is the production of hit records. Where else can a musician get paid so well for doing something he loves to do, and also hear himself every time he switches on a radio or flips a television channel?

* * *

REFERENCE MATERIALS

Aebersold, Jamey— *A New Approach to Jazz Improvisation*
Scales For Jazz Improvisation
Recorded Series—New Albany, Indiana

Anderson, Doug— *Jazz and Show Choir Handbook*
Hinshaw Music, Inc.
Chapel Hill, North Carolina

Baker, Mickey— *Jazz Guitar, Book I*
Lewis Publishing Co.

Baker, David— *Advanced Improvisation*
Techniques of Improvisation Series
Jazz Improvisation
Music Workshop Publication, Chicago, Illinois

Brown, Ray— *Bass Method*
First Place Music Publications
Studio City, California

Burns, Roy— *Drum Set Artistry*—Book & Record
Alfred Publishing Co., Inc.
Sherman Oaks, California

Carter, Ron— *Building a Jazz Bass Line*
Ronald Carter Music Co.
New York, New York

Carubia, Michael— *The Sound of Improvisation*—
Individual & Group
Jazz Rock & You—Individual & Group
Alfred Publishing Co., Inc.
Sherman Oaks, California

Coker, Jerry— *Improvising Jazz and The Jazz Idiom*
Prentice Hall, Inc., Englewood Cliffs, New Jersey

Cross, David &
DeMiero, Frank— *Vocal Jazz Riffs*
Michael Kysar Publishing, Seattle, Washington

Delamont, George— *Modern Arranging Techniques*
Kendor Music, Delevan, New York

DeMiero, Frank— *Vocal Jazz Ornamentation and Inflection*
Michael Kysar Publications, Seattle, Washington

Dobbins, Bill—   *The Contemporary Jazz Pianist*
                        GAMT Music Press, Jamestown, Rhode Island

Downbeat Magazine— Chicago, Illinois

Farber, Mitchell—   *Rock and Pop Chord Progressions*
                            (with cassette)
                        Alfred Publishing Co., Inc.
                        Sherman Oaks, California

Feldstein, Sandy &
Scianni, Joseph—   *The Sound of Rock*—method book
                        Alfred Publishing Co., Inc.
                        Sherman Oaks, California

Ferguson, Tom—   *Instant Improvisation at The Piano*
                        Alfred Publishing Co., Inc.
                        Sherman Oaks, California

Fink, Ron—   *Drum Set Reading*
                        Alfred Publishing Co., Inc.
                        Sherman Oaks, California

Green, Ted—   *Chord Chemistry*
                        DZ Publications, Canoga Park, California

Friedman, Laura &
Coryell, Julie—   *Jazz-Rock Fusion*
                        Delta, New York

Gridley, Mark—   *Jazz Styles*
                        Prentice-Hall, New York

Grove, Dick—   *Theory of Improvisation*
                        First Place Music, Studio City, California

Haerle, Dan—   *Jazz/Rock Voicings for the Contemporary
                            Keyboard Player*
                        Studio P.R., Lebanon, Indiana

Jazz Magazine—   P. O. Box 212, Northport, New York

Joyce, Jim—   *A Guide to Writing Vocal Arrangements*
                        First Place Music, Studio City, California

Kaye, Carol—   *Electric Bass Lines*
                        GWYN Publications, Sherman Oaks, California

Kerr, Anita—   *Voices*
                       MCA Music, New York

Kinkle, Roger—   *The Complete Encyclopedia of Popular*
                           Music and Jazz
                       Nostalgia Book Club (Arlington House)
                       New Rochelle, New York

Konowitz, Bert—   *Vocal Improvisation Method*
                       Alfred Publishing Co., Inc.
                       Sherman Oaks, California

Kraintz, Ken—   *Vocal Jazz Warm Ups*
                       Michael Kysar Publications, Seattle, Washington

Kysar, Michael—   *Vocal Jazz Concepts for the Music Educator*

LaPorta, John—   *Guide to Improvisation*
                       Berklee Press, Boston, Massachusetts

Levey, Joseph—   *Basic Jazz Improvisation*
                       Shawnee Press
                       Deleware Water Gap, Pennsylvania

Mancini, Henry—   *Sounds And Scores*
                       Northridge Music Co., Northridge, California

Mehegan, John—   *John Mehegan Improvisation Series*
                       Watson-Guptill, New York

                       Studies in Jazz Harmony
                       Styles for the Jazz Pianist
                       Carl Fischer, Chicago, Illinois

Music Minus One—   A variety of play and sing along recordings
                       New York

N.A.J.E. Educator—   Magazine of the National Association
                           of Jazz Educators

Owens, Tom—   *Charlie Parker: Techniques of*
                           Improvisation, Vol. 1 & 2
                       Zerox University Microfilms
                       300 N. Zeeb Road, Ann Arbor, Michigan

Reid, Rufus—   *The Evolving Bassist*
                       Myriad, Ltd., New York

Rizzo, Phil—   *Spread Chord Voicing*
                       Modern Music School, Cleveland, Ohio

                       Modern Music Theory Text
                       Jazz Education Press, Manhattan, Kansas

Ritz, David &
Charles, Ray—   *Brother Ray: Ray Charles' Own Story*
                       Dial Press, New York

Roemer, Clint—   *Standarized Chord Symbol Notation*
                       Sherman Oaks, California

Russell, George—   *Lydian Chromatic Concept*
                       Concept Publishing Co., New York

Sebesky, Don—   *The Contemporary Arranger*
                       Alfred Publishing Co., Inc.
                       Sherman Oaks, California

Shaw, Kirby—   *Vocal Jazz Style*
                       Hal Leonard Publishing

Smalley, Jack—   *A Simplified Guide to Writing and
                         Arranging for Swing and Show Choirs and
                         Small Instrumental Groups*
                       First Place Music, Studio City, California

Spera, Dominick—   *Learning Unlimited Jazz
                         Improvisation Series*
                       Hal Leonard Publications

Strommen, Carl &
Feldstein, Sandy—   *The Sound of Jazz*—method
                       Alfred Publishing Co., Inc.
                       Sherman Oaks, California

Tilles, Bob—   *Practical Improvisations*
                       Belwin-Mills, New York

Wheaton, Jack—   *Basic Modal Improvisation Techniques
                         for Keyboard Instruments*
                       First Place Music, Studio City, California

DISCOGRAPHY

ARTIST	TITLE	LABEL
Allison, Mose	Seventh Son	Prestige 10052
	I Don't Worry About a Thing	Atlantic 1389
	Doin' Some Thinkin'	Atlantic S–1542
	The Best Of	Atlantic SD–1542
	Your Mind is on Vacation	Atlantic SD–1691
Anderson, Ernestine	Hello Like Before	Concord CJ–31
Baker, Chet	Sings & Plays Billie Holiday	Trip 5569
Basie, Count	With Joe Williams	Verve 68488
	With Sarah Vaughn	Roulette 42016
Bennett, Tony with Bill Evans	Together Again	Improv 7117
Benson, George	Breezin'	Warner 2919
Blood Sweat & Tears	More Than	Columbia PC–34233
	New Blood	Columbia MC–31790
	Greatest Hits	Columbia PC–31170
	Blood Sweat & Tears	Columbia PC–9720
	Child is Father to the Man	Columbia CS–9619
Bread	Lost Without	Elektra 1094
Bridgewater, Dee Dee	Dee Dee Bridgewater	Atlantic 18188
Brown, Oscar Jr.	Movin' On	Atlantic 1629
Cain, Jackie: Kral, Roy	Jackie Cain & Roy Kral	Brunswick BI–54026
	A Wilder Alias	CTI 6040
	Time and Love	CTI 6019
	Concert by The Sea	Studio 7–402

Carter, Betty	Inside Betty Carter	U.S. UAS–5639
	What a Little Moonlight	Impulse 9321
Charles, Ray & Cleo Laine	Porgy & Bess	RCA CPL 2–1831
Chicago	Chicago X	Columbia PC–34200
	Hits	Columbia PC–33900
	Chicago	Columbia PC–24
	Transit Authority	Columbia PG–8
Coleman, Earl	A Song For You	Xanadu 147
Conner, Chris	Sketches	Stanyan 10029
Corea, Chick	Leprechaun	Polydor PD–6062
Curb, Mike (Congregation)	Put Your Hand in the Hand	MGM SE–4785
Double Six of Paris	Double Six	Philips PHM–200106
	with Dizzy Gillespie	Philips PHM–200106
	Swingin' & Singin'	Philips PHM–200026
	sing Ray Charles	Philips PHM–200141
Fifth Dimension	Age of Aquarious	Soul City SCS–92005
	Greatest Hits on Earth	Bell 1106
	Individually & Collectively	Bell 6073
	The July 5th Album	Soul City SCS–33911
	Earthbound	ABC 897
	Stoned Soul Picnic	Soul City SCS–92002
	Up, Up and Away	Soul City SCS–92000
Fitzgerald, Ella	At the Montreaux Jazz Festival	Pablo 2310–751
	with Duke Ellington at the Cote D'Azur	Verve V6–4072–2
	Live at Carnegie Hall	Columbia KG–32557
	Newport Jazz Festival	Verve 6–8826
	Take Love Easy (with Joe Pass)	Pablo 2310–702
Flack, Roberta	Chapter Two	Atlantic
	First Take	Atlantic
	Quiet Fire	Atlantic
	Feel Like Makin' Love	Atlantic

Four Freshman	Best	CAP SY–4562
	Different Strokes	Liberty LST–7630
	with Kenton & Christy Live at Butler University	Creative World ST–1059
	and Five Trombones	Cap. SM–11639
Free Design	Kites are Fun	Project 3 PR–5037sd
	There is a Song	Kendor Publications
	One by One	Project 3 PR–4006sd
	You Could Be Born Again	Project 3 PR–5031sd
Gentle Giant	Free Hand	Capitol ST–11428
	Interview	Capitol ST–11532
	Acquiring the Taste	Vertigo VEL–1005
Hi-Lo's	Love Nest	Columbia CL–1121
	Suddenly	Columbia CL–952
	Under Glass	Under Starlite 7005
Holiday, Billie	Essential	Verve V6–8410
	God Bless The Child	Columbia G–30782
Horne, Lena	with Gabor Szabo	Buddah 5669
	with Michel Legrand	RCA BGLI–1026
Jarreau, Al	All Fly Home	Warner BSK–3229
Jones, Quincy	Sounds, & Stuff Like That	A & M SP–4685
Anita Kerr Singers	It's Anita Kerr Country	Dot DLP–25976
	Reflect	Dot DLP–25906
King, B. B.	Friends	ABC 825
	Lucille Talks Back	ABC 898
King, Morgana	Stretchin' Out	Muse MR–5166
King Pleasure	The Source	Prestige PR–24017
Kral, Irene	Gentle Rain	Choice CRS–1020
Laine, Cleo	Born Friday	RCA LPLI–5113
	At Carnegie Hall	RCA LPLI–5013

Lambert, Hendricks & Ross	The Best of LH & R	Columbia KC–32911
	Hottest New Group in Jazz	Columbia CS–8198
	Sing a Song Of Basie	ABC PAR–223
	Sing Ellington	Columbia CL–1510
	Way Out Voices	Odyssey C3216–0292
Manhattan Transfer	Manhattan Transfer	At. SD–18133
	Coming Out	At. SD–18183
McRae, Carmen	Just a Little Lovin'	AT SD–1568
	Sound of Silence	AT 8200
	Take Five (with Brubeck)	CSP JCS–9116
	I am Music	United Artists
Mendes, Sergio	Love Music	Bell 1119
	Home Cooking	Elektra 1055
Mount Hood Community College Vocal Jazz Ensemble	Walk Softly Send in the Clowns Mt. Hood C.C.	Creative World Campus Store,
Mangione, Chuck (with Esther Satterfield & Horseheads Chamber Singers	Land of Make Believe	Mercury SRM–1–684
O'Day, Anita	Berlin Jazz Festival 1970	BASF 20750
Pointer Sisters	That's a Plenty	Blue Thumb 6009
	Anita, Ruth, Jane, Bonnie	Blue Thumb
	Steppin'	Blue Thumb 6021
	Live at The Opera House	Blue Thumb
Quire	Quire is a Choir	RCA BGL 1–1700
Rankin, Kenny	The Kenny Rankin Album	
	with Don Costa	Little David 1013
	Inside	Little David 1009
	Like a Seed	Little David 1003
	Silver Morning	Little David 3000
Rushing, Jimmy	Good Morning Blues (with Helen Humes)	MCA 2–4108

Satterfield, Esther	Need to Be .	A & M 3411
	Once I Loved	A & M 3408
Simone, Nina	Baltimore	CTI 7084
	Nina Simone	Up Front 145
	Songs of the Poets	RCA 1–1788
	Here Comes the Sun	RCA 4536
	The Best of	Philips 600–298
	Little Girl Blue	BCP 6082
Sinatra, Frank	Sinatra and Basie	Reprise FS–1008
	at the Sands with	
	Quincy Jones	Reprise 1019
	Francis A. &	
	Edward K.	Reprise FS–1024
Singers Unlimited	A Capella	BASF 20903
	A Capella 2	BASF 22343
	Feeling Free	BASF 22607
	Sentimental Journey	BASF 22335
	In Tune with	
	Oscar Peterson	BASF 20905
	Try to Remember	BASF 20903
Sound of Feeling	with Oliver Nelson	Verve V6–8743
Stan Kenton	Artistry in	
	Voices and Brass	Creative World 1038
Snow, Phoebe	Second Childhood	Columbia PC–34387
Starland Vocal Band	Wind	BHL 1–1351
Swingle Singers	Bach's Hits	PHI 600097
	Any one for Mozart?	PHS 600149
	Going Baroque	PHS 600126
	Madrigals & Madriguys	Columbia PC–34194
	Joy of Singing	PHS 700004
Torme, Mel	Live at the Maisonette	Atlantic 18129
	That's All	CSP EN–13090
	Back in Town	
	(with the Meltones)	Verve 2120
	with the Meltones &	
	Artie Shaw	Everest FS–324
Vaughn, Sarah	Feeling Good	Mainstream 404
	Golden Hits	Mercury 60645
	Live in Japan	Mainstream 401

	Send in the Clowns	Mainstream 412
	with Michel Legrand	Mainstream 361
Washington, Dinah	Queen of the Blues	Roulette RE–117
Williams, Joe	Basie Swings, Williams Sings	Verve V/V6–8488
	Live with Cannonball Adderly	Fantasy 9441
	the Best of	Up Front 161
Wilson, Nancy	Nancy Wilson Show with George Shearing	Capitol SKAC–2136
Vocal Jazz Celebration	high school & college jazz vocal ensembles	Hinshaw Music, Box 470, Chapel Hill N.C. 27514
Vocal Jazz, Inc.	High Clouds	Grapevine Records GVR 3310 Grenadilla Ent. 345 Park Ave. N.Y., NY 10010